# Volunteers in the African Bush
## Memoirs from Sierra Leone

*For Wally and Celeta*
*Some memories*
*from days past*
*Wayne 2013*

### Edited by David Read Barker

dog ear
PUBLISHING

First published by Dog Ear Publishing
4010 W. 86th Street, Ste H
Indianapolis, IN 46268
www.dogearpublishing.net

ISBN: 978-1-4575-1618-4

This book is printed on acid-free paper.

Printed in the United States of America

# Contents

# Foreword

*Dr. Joseph C. Kennedy*

*Dr. Joseph C. Kennedy was the Peace Corps director for Sierra Leone from 1967 to 1969 and in 1972 co-founded Africare, a nonprofit organization that has raised $1.5 billion to improve the quality of life of Africans.*

A dream, a hope, a belief—Peace Corps.

I was in Nigeria when President Kennedy announced the creation of the Peace Corps with the dynamic, energetic Sargent Shriver to lead it. A number of Nigerian officials asked what I thought. Could Americans, young or old, go to countries around the world and help people to a better life? I replied, yes, I believed they could.

Later, on reflecting, I wondered if they really could. I was finishing a year of research that had taken me into remote towns and villages in Liberia, Ghana, and Nigeria. How would Peace Corps volunteers deal with the 110–115-degree heat with no air conditioning, long rainy seasons where everything floods and long dry seasons where everything withers and dies, and diseases such as malaria, carried by mosquitoes? How could they deal with sights of people living in poverty, not having enough to eat, no clean water to drink, of children and adults dying young from curable diseases? How could they deal with unfamiliar cultures and languages, strange foods, and certainly, for many, being a racial minority for the first time? Could Americans who had never traveled around the United States, or even out of their own state, go to the distant lands of Africa, Asia, the South Pacific, and South America? Could they survive and make a positive contribution to the people in these countries?

The answer was a resounding yes. In November 2011 the Peace Corps celebrated its 50th anniversary. During the first half century, more than 200,000 volunteers had served in 139 countries, 3,567 of them in Sierra Leone. There were successes and failures, but they made a positive contribution. On returning to the United States, they became teachers, writers, doctors, college presidents, and staff in organizations such as CARE, Save the Children, and Africare.

*Volunteers in the African Bush* relates the experiences of 25 Peace Corps volunteers, part of a group of 76 volunteers who served in Sierra Leone in 1965–67, only the third group to serve there. These 25 were designated Chiefdom Development or Community Development volunteers and were sent to work in rural areas of the country–the bush.

There were several married couples, in which the men were to work with farmers to improve farming techniques, to build roads and bridges, and to dig wells. The volunteer women worked with the village women on nutrition, including matters such as boiling their water and breast feeding. Some volunteers were placed individually, isolated in places where maybe only one or two of the local people spoke English. All were caught up in unfamiliar languages (although each volunteer had language training), customs, and foods. Their living conditions were rudimentary: no running water, no electricity, and an outdoor latrine that was often just a hole in the ground. They were plagued by a lack of equipment and, some said, a lack of adequate training.

Their respite came occasionally when they could go to the capital, Freetown, for a checkup by the Peace Corps doctor and the chance to visit the local bars and view the lovely Lumley Beach, which overlooks the Atlantic Ocean.

There were many individual experiences. Many unfortunately were exposed to *tiefmen* who broke into their houses at night. Some were exposed to the mysterious magical power of the witchdoctors.

Most of the villagers were, by western standards, living in poverty. Men and women dug in their fields, bending low with short-handled hoes; there were no tractors. Women worked with babies on their backs, buckets on their heads, walking to streams to bathe, wash clothes, and bring back water to drink. Children died young. Yet in spite of it all, the volunteers persevered. They could laugh and sing and dance. Enjoying life was not bound by material wealth. Also, for many, leisure time—free time—was more important than additional money, and finally, time itself was not measured by a clock or a watch, but by broad times of morning, afternoon, evening, and night.

There were successes and failures. Looking back, some volunteers wondered if they had really made a difference in the lives of the people. Some wondered if in some way they had contributed to the turmoil that would later beset Sierra Leone.

Today, in 2012, there are 9,000 Peace Corps volunteers serving in 75 countries. Is there still a need for the Peace Corps? Around the world, millions of people still go to sleep hungry. Thousands die from curable diseases. Children die in infancy. There is lack of education, lack of equality. There is turmoil and lack of peace. There is, indeed, a call for the Peace Corps.

# Introduction

*David Read Barker*

It is hard to read Ishmael Beah's memoir, *A Long Way Gone*, without a gut-wrenching feeling of horror at what it meant to be a boy soldier in Sierra Leone's long civil war. His story gave me several nights of bad dreams. "What," I wondered, "if our work as Peace Corps Volunteers actually contributed to the chaos that descended on Sierra Leone a quarter-century after we left? After all, our Peace Corps bosses routinely called us "Agents of Change." Perhaps we had unwittingly planted the seeds of the Revolutionary United Front, which introduced the world to the novelty of "be-handing." Could it be that our work exemplified the adage that "The road to Hell is paved with good intentions?" Or were these thoughts merely the residual guilt of a senior citizen whose country had subsequently fought too many wars to promote freedom around the world?

Over the following weeks, I couldn't shake the dream's question, which persisted and grew to the point that it compelled me to check up with the other Peace Corps Volunteers in my group, which was assigned to Sierra Leone from 1965 to 1967.

Our Peace Corps group was known by at least two names: "Rural and Agricultural Development" and "Chiefdom Development." The two names reflected parallel strategies and personnel. It began, in August 1965, with 20 married couples, 42 single men, and seven single women. The married couples were all young; the wives ranged in age from 19 to 26, and the husbands were from 21 to 28. Most had been married less than three months. The single men were also very young; five were still teenagers, and the youngest was only 17. By far the oldest man, an insurance salesman from New York, was 32. The single women ranged in age from 20 to 26 with the exception of the "grandmother" of the group, a 42-year-old dairy farmer from New York.

Training was carried out at Hampton Institute, in Hampton, Virginia, and at the recently opened Peace Corps training center located at

"Profit," in St. Croix, U.S. Virgin Islands. Hampton Institute, a historically black college, now known as Hampton University, had been an early applicant to train a Peace Corps group, but the first contracts had gone to better-known universities such as Michigan and Yale. Ours was the first Peace Corps group to be trained at Hampton Institute. During the course of the 15-week-long training program, a total of nine people were "deselected" by the Peace Corps staff, four people quit, and one person was added to the group, so a total of 76 people took up assignments in Sierra Leone in early January 1966.

The plan, as we understood it, was to place the married couples in chiefdom headquarters towns, generally more remote places where they could provide companionship to one another. The husbands were expected to support civil works and agricultural extension, while the wives were to work on nutrition, basic medical care, and education. Some of the single men were posted to a total of 10 of the 12 district capitals in Sierra Leone. They were provided with four-wheel drive vehicles and expected to support civil works projects throughout the district. The rest of the single men were assigned specific agricultural extension or construction jobs in villages and towns throughout the country. Nearly all of the single women were posted to the larger towns to carry out nutrition and nutrition education programs.

Within a few days after arriving in Sierra Leone, we were dispersed across the country and almost never saw one another again, except by happenstance in the Peace Corps rest house in Freetown, the capital, on shopping and R&R visits. A conference on upland rice was held at Njala, in March 1966, and an agricultural training session for some in the group was held at Rokupr in early 1967.

Reciprocating hospitality was a pillar of the Peace Corps ethos, and it is an often-repeated theme in the accounts collected here. But there was no mechanism, then or after the period of volunteer service ended, for people to keep in touch with one another. A few friends maintained occasional contacts for decades, but in general everyone lost touch with everyone else.

Fast-forward 45 years. The few sustained contacts, supplemented by the search engine algorithms of Google and WhitePages.com, facilitated the rediscovery of 53 members of the group of 76. Among the 23 people who had not been traced as of this writing are people with very common names, several women who have remarried and taken new names, and a few people who for their own reasons seem not to want to be in contact with others from their Peace Corps experience.

Of the 53 former Peace Corps Volunteers in the Sierra Leone 1965–67 group about whom definite information was obtained, eight have died since completing their period of volunteer service. The 25 authors of this book therefore make up slightly more than half of all those who could be contacted. Nine were single men when they served in the Peace Corps, four were married couples who are still married, and seven were married but have since been divorced, or a spouse has passed away. Unfortunately, none of the seven single women have written for this book.

In the mid-1960s, Sierra Leone was divided into four administrative districts, sometimes referred to as provinces: Western, comprising the national capital, Freetown, and its immediate suburbs; Southern, whose capital was the town of Bo; Eastern, whose capital was the town of Kenema; and Northern, whose capital was the town of Makeni. The Southern Region was further divided into four districts: Pujehun, with headquarters in the town of Pujehun; Moyamba, with headquarters in the town of Moyamba; Bonthe, with headquarters in the town of Bonthe; and Bo, with headquarters in Bo. The Eastern Region was divided into three districts: Kenema, with headquarters in Kenema; Kono, with headquarters in Koidu Town, sometimes also referred to as Sefadu; and Kailahun, with headquarters in the town of Kailahun. The Northern Region was divided into five districts: Port Loko, with headquarters in Port Loko; Tonkolili, with headquarters in Magburaka; Koinadugu, with headquarters in Kabala; Bombali, with headquarters in the provincial capital of Makeni; and Kambia, with headquarters in the town of Kambia.

Sierra Leone: Regions and districts

3

The Peace Corps volunteers whose essays appear in this book were posted in all four administrative regions and in 10 of the 12 districts; only Bonthe, in the south, and Tonkolili, in the north, are not represented here. The 21 chapters are arranged geographically, from south to north. The map below shows the locations of the volunteers' posts, keyed to the chapter numbers in the Contents.

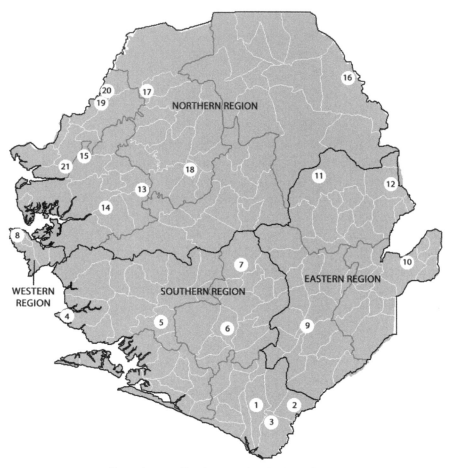

Sierra Leone: Regions and volunteers' posts

# Key to Map

## Southern Region
### Pujehun District

1. Wayne Walther — Pujehun Town
2. Richard Pflugfelder — Zimmi, Makpele Chiefdom
3. Bill and Barbara Coats — Blama, Gallinas-Perri Chiefdom

### Moyamba District

4. Susie Getzschman — Shenge, Kagboro Chiefdom
5. John and Betty Wuesthoff — Sembehun, Bagruna Chiefdom

### Bo District

6. Barry H. Hill — Telu, Jaiama-Bongor Chiefdom
7. Stephen M. Bingham — Njama, Kowa Chiefdom

## Western Region

8. Judy and Dwight Sandlin — Freetown

## Eastern Region

### Kenema District

9. Doc Long — Kenema Town

### Kailahun District

10. Milton Lane — Kailahun Town

## Kono District

11. Rev. John H. Cole — Kayima, Sando Chiefdom
12. Roger B. Hirschland — Saiama, Lei Chiefdom

## Northern Region

### Port Loko District

13. Tom Cook — Rokel, Marampa Chiefdom
14. Len Aitken — Masimera, Masimera Chiefdom
15. Charles & Moira Geoffrion — Mange-Bureh Chiefdom

### Koinadugu District

16. Randy Cummings — Mongo Chiefdom

### Bombali District

17. Robert Galeria — Tambaka Chiefdom
18. Gerry Cashion — Makeni Town

### Kambia District

19. David Read Barker — Kukuna, Bramaia Chiefdom
20. Judith Kimmes Barker — Kukuna, Bramaia Chiefdom
21. Tom Crum — Samu Chiefdom

This book is an answer to my nagging dream's question. Almost every one of the 25 authors of this book experienced events that were frightening and inexplicable, but none make any claim to having foreseen the ferocity of the civil war in Sierra Leone. Although the Peace Corps as an institution comes in for many hard knocks in the following accounts, the volunteer idealism that John Kennedy inspired carried many of us through loneliness, sickness, and isolation to produce life-altering experiences.

There is a Glossary at the end.

I wish to give thanks to my wife Lisa Borre for her unfailing encouragement and for making the maps. I acknowledge with great thanks the authors of these collected essays and especially to Roger B. Hirschland, Charles A. Geoffrion, and Susie Getzschman, all of whom are members of our Peace Corps group, for their insightful comments and many editorial corrections. Thanks also to Tom Cook for the cover photo.

# I

# Southern Region

## 1.

## Life Along the Waanje

*Wayne Walther*

My mother cried at the airport when I left West Texas after Christmas 1965 to join up with my Peace Corps group headed for Sierra Leone. She was not the weepy sort, and her crying disturbed me. I wanted to comfort her by saying, "It's going to be all right. I'm only going six or seven thousand miles away and I'll be back in a couple of years." We were heading for New York City, where several of us met up, and thanks to Larry Arato, our Brooklyn volunteer, we stayed a few days, ate fabulous Italian food, and saw "Hello, Dolly" on Broadway. The tickets were an astronomical $9.50. We enjoyed the spectacle of a New York transit strike, pooling taxi rides, walking, and finally catching the charter plane to Conakry, Guinea.

After the plane was airborne and cans of beer had been liberally distributed, we experienced some "turbulence" at which the pilot insisted that everyone be seated and buckled up. Some of the more worldly-wise among us suggested that the pilot had himself caused the dip and sway in order to avoid the possibility of a wild party at 20,000 feet, but I was not one to know the difference. I was still largely in awe of most of the other members of our group, who in training had seemed more aware of the world than I. One of our speakers from Washington had complimented our group for having so many volunteers who had had the "benefit of an East Coast education." I was only mildly offended by the remark at the time. We had not yet had the national reckoning of the depths to which the "best and brightest" of that well-educated generation would lead us in Southeast Asia. And I counted myself lucky to be with such a smart and handsome group of people, heading for a true international adventure.

Training had been both trying and exciting at the same time. Reading some of the diary I kept at the time, I am surprised by the amount of drinking we did, by the frustrations some of us felt at inadequate language preparation, and by the anxieties we experienced about the process known as de-selection. It was a strange process by which individuals and couples were informed that for various reasons they would not be going to Sierra Leone with the rest of the group. There were three rounds of de-selection, the last one in the Virgin Islands, just before we all went home for Christmas at the end of our training. But most of the time I was happy to be there, happy to meet so many people from so many places, happy to talk to folks who clearly had ambition and adventure on their minds. Texas in the 1960s was a fairly provincial place intellectually, and it was bracing to meet people who had such different backgrounds and ideas. Even more remarkable to me was the unity we all felt, the sense that we were doing something to remake the world, to make a difference and bring a measure of health and happiness and wholeness to places that could use some American energy. I think most of us also understood and accepted the second goal of the Peace Corps; we were also going there to learn from our interactions with others. Finding health and happiness and wholeness for ourselves was probably a larger part of our agendas than we usually acknowledged.

So we flew to Conakry, transferred to a smaller USSR-built plane for the short flight to Freetown, and then landed to a blast of hot tropical air, so radically different from the New York and West Texas air I'd recently been breathing. There is something peculiar about the odor of a tropical city, a mixture of humidity and diesel exhaust and exotic fruits. It is so distinctive that whenever I have since traveled even to Mexico, I still remember the first smell of Freetown that excites and warns me and says, "Be careful, you're on unfamiliar ground here."

It took us a week or two in Freetown to get our assignments and transportation to our new posts, and all of it was designed, I suppose, gradually to introduce us to African ways and African experience. I ended up, with Dick Pflugfelder and John Root, in the care of Harry Hogan, whose group was scheduled to leave Sierra Leone a month or so later. If Harry had reservations about the new kids coming in to take over the work he had begun in the Pujehun District, he was smart enough not to say anything. I remember coming in to the house where we were to live for the next two years and seeing a bare light bulb hanging from its cord in the middle of the living room. We had a large house with electricity 18 hours a day, so we were really very comfortable. But I said to Harry, "That light will have to go. It's just too harsh." He laughed and said, "Well, if you really want to get rid of it, do it quickly, in the next week or two. Otherwise, you'll get used to it and never change it." When we left 20 months later, the bare light bulb was still hanging from its wire in the middle of the living room. I wonder how much of our rural development work was like that light bulb. We spent a lot of time looking around, talking to folks, thinking about projects and work that we should have and could have and would have done, but by the time we figured out what the problems were and how we might organize to address them, they had become part of the scenery, we had gotten used to things the way they were, and we were immobilized by the familiarity of it all.

We were a rural development group—not a teacher group, as most volunteers in Sierra Leone were at that time. Our mission in Sierra Leone was to work with African counterparts in building infrastructure projects using local labor and materials from either Sierra Leone government sources or sometimes from USAID. Most of the projects involved roads and bridges and school houses. We were trained as agricultural advisors, particularly in the growing of newer varieties of rice that were more productive than the traditional types planted by Africans. I think that part of our training was mostly academic, and not much was used. At one point I did receive a shipment of a few bags of improved rice seeds, and these were distributed in a couple of chiefdoms, but I never knew what became of them or if they were better or not.

Along with the carpenter at the boys high school in Pujehun, I managed to build a two-room classroom using a pre-fabricated steel frame from USAID and bricks made by the school workmen using a CINVA ram mold, a nifty little device that used local clay, a little cement, and lots of "sweat equity" to make bricks that dried and cured in the African sun. The bricks were solid, gray, and a little clunky, but they worked well, and could be laid fairly easily. I always marveled at the convent built about 1910 for the Polish nuns who had established a girls school in Pujehun. Those bricks were a rich golden color, absolutely uniform, and perfectly laid. The buildings were elegant in their simplicity and ingenuity, using large porches and high windows to provide second-story breezes to the women serving the African mission there. I marveled, too, at the local Anglican Church, built of handsome local stone about 1900. This was amazing to me, when I realized that the town of Pujehun was being established as a trading post and mission center about the same time that my little town of Rowena, in West Texas, was being settled on the Santa Fe railroad. Somehow it surprised me that this African church was older than the little U.C.C. congregation I grew up in.

My contribution to Catholic education in Pujehun was, with the aid of the local prison inmates, leveling a section of the yard for a tennis court. The boys had their own tennis courts, and the Europeans (who included Peace Corps volunteers) and local officials used the concrete court in the middle of town, a remnant of colonial days. For a few weeks during the rainy season, I also filled in to teach Sierra Leone geography to one of the girls' classes. Building a bridge at Kalu, a couple of roads and school buildings, and a tennis court, were probably the quantifiable part of my work in Sierra Leone.

I suffered from not knowing what to do. From Harry I took over a couple of bridge projects close to little towns that needed them to open up areas cut off during the rainy season. I worked with a counterpart from the district council, who mostly humored me, I think, but with whom I did accomplish a few things. Eventually I realized that my counterpart knew a lot more than I did about building forms, pouring concrete, and organizing work gangs, and that I would be wise to step back and let him do those things. I have always been grateful to have lived among and worked with Muslim people. Especially in the past 10 years, it has been good to be able to say that I worked closely and comfortably with a Muslim counterpart and that all was well. Certainly those were simpler times, but if it happened then, why not now?

What I brought to the projects, which my counterpart lacked, was a Western understanding of bureaucracy and the ability to talk to people in the ministries in Bo and Freetown in order to get supplies moving in the right direction. And I had a truck to get us to work and back. But I was never sure of what my job was supposed to be or what I could reasonably expect others to do to help. Once, I drove in frustration to

Freetown to talk to the Peace Corps director about a particularly problematic phase of bridge construction. I had taken over a project that my predecessor had begun, a bridge in Kalu, not far from Pujehun, where I lived. It was a little larger than anything I had ever done before, and even at that, I had wondered if it were large enough and long enough to allow the flow of rainy season water to pass through. I really wanted some technical guidance on bridge design.

So I made an appointment, and the Peace Corps director was very concerned; he asked questions and let me talk about the project. About 15 minutes into the interview, it dawned on me that of all the people in Sierra Leone, I knew more about this bridge project than anyone else, and although I did not know what I was going to do next, no one else knew what to do either, and I would likely be the only one who would find out what to do and then do it. And so, haltingly and inefficiently, I did. I should say, we did, my counterpart and I and the people who showed up periodically to work.

A funny thing happened as we were building this bridge in Kalu. First, I learned that you should always start at the farthest end when you build roads in the bush. That way, volunteer workers will stay with you until the road is finished. If you start from the town and work outward, many volunteers will work only until the road reaches their farm, and then they become much less available when the call to work goes out. The culmination of this project was a bridge that crossed a little stream that ran beside the town. Even small children could easily step over the creek during the dry season, but during the rainy season it swelled to a 30-foot-wide, 10-foot-deep river. We were planning a concrete-and-steel bridge that could carry vehicles as well as foot traffic. When we had progressed far enough to have completed the bridge abutments, we needed to lay the steel framework for the road from one side to the other. These were huge contraptions, I think military surplus, that could be bolted together to form quick bridges in combat zones. That was all well and good, but we had no crane, no tractor, nothing to handle what were probably thousand-pound lengths of steel. So we sat together one day and talked about what the bridge would look like, two frames bolted together, stretched from one abutment to the other for one track and an identical pair beside it for the other track. We all agreed what it would look like when it was finished, but no one, and certainly not I, had any idea of how to get them in place. I left that afternoon completely puzzled, and went to Freetown for a few days for some other project, and it was a week or two before I returned to the work site to continue puzzling out this work problem. I was amazed when I drove up to find the bridge frame completed, the two parallel tracks of steel lying exactly as we had talked about. I was impressed, and congratulated the workers on their job, and we celebrated. Somehow I thought it best not to ask how they actually had done it. Sometimes it may be better not to know the details.

I mentioned the truck. I inherited it from Harry, who had gotten it from someone who worked with CARE, which was contracted to oversee our Peace Corps group. The truck was an old Land Rover that Harry had named Rocinante, after Don Quixote's horse. Rocinante was sometimes fickle but never failed to get us where we were going. An old Lebanese mechanic in Bo periodically wired it and worked to keep it running. For a long time Rocinante had no battery, so I always backed up to the house, since the driveway was slightly inclined toward the street. In the morning, our cook and houseboy would follow me outside and give me a little push to get it started. It never failed. Finding folks to give me a push start was seldom a problem at the worksite. Dead batteries were not unheard of in the bush. It was only difficult when I thoughtlessly parked in the sand. Once, on the way to Bo, Rocinante stopped dead, and none of us aboard could figure out what had happened. My traveling companions caught the next lorry in, while I puzzled a bit, until I figured the problem was electrical, and reattached the lead wire to the distributor with adhesive tape from the first aid kit. For days following, I prided myself on my "Peace Corps ingenuity." Another time on the road to Freetown, a passing lorry tossed a rock into the windshield, which was made of tempered glass, and we watched over a period of five or ten seconds as the windshield shattered into perfect nickel sized crystals, like a screen dissolving into frost. It was fascinating and absorbing, except that this was all taking place on a two-lane highway traveling 50 or 60 miles per hour. Rocinante finally died of a blown head gasket and was replaced by a brand new Chevy four-wheel-drive truck, one of a half dozen or so our group received sometime halfway through our time in country. The truck was great, bigger and more comfortable, but it never had the personality of the Land Rover. I never got around to painting Rocinante II on the door.

Life was good in Pujehun, except when it wasn't. We had a few African friends, but mostly we socialized with the other PCVs in town, Michelle, Dianne, and Amy, who were teachers at the Catholic Boys and Girls High School. We also spent time with the Holy Ghost Fathers, the Irish priests who served the local parish as well as the boys school. Irish nuns ran the girls school. We knew them also, but not as well. There were also contract teachers from Ireland, England, Ceylon, and India. My experience, consequently, was more international than African. Sometimes I thought the couples and single PCVs who were located in smaller towns had a richer African experience, in that they were forced to socialize more with Africans, but I'm not sure. John Root was stationed in a small town on the road to Bo from the beginning, and Richard Pflugfelder moved about midway through our time in-country to a small town on the way to Zimmi, the headquarters town of the Makpele Chiefdom. I stayed in Pujehun, the provincial capital, where the other volunteers were a great support group and good friends to spend time with.

I got sick about halfway through my time in Sierra Leone. The Peace Corps doctor whom I saw a few weeks later said it sounded like I had dengue fever: high temperature, severe headaches for a couple of days, then no symptoms. The doctor said that if it was dengue fever, I might experience some depression in three or four weeks. That often happens after a bout of dengue fever, and of course, it did in my case. I was glad to be warned, because then when I became depressed, I could at least understand that it wasn't just the heat or the job or my frustration and inefficiency–it was the mosquitoes. The support of the teacher volunteers was crucial during the next couple of months until I came around. Somehow they put up with me and fed me and encouraged me. That experience has made me more able to accept others dealing with depression. I usually tell them my Africa story and the connection between changes in body chemistry and depression, and somehow that comforts others suffering from it.

A few weeks into the depression, I was staying home most days, because I couldn't plan to do anything and didn't feel like doing anything even if I had wanted to, which I didn't. So I thought I would try painting to lift my spirits. A gay college friend of mine had given me a nice set of water colors when he learned I was going into the Peace Corps. He said he figured I would have lots of time on my hands and might enjoy doing water colors as a way to pass the time. He had left a little note taped to the top of the box of colors: "May all your days be as bright as these colors!" That was a fine sentiment. Well, the day I decided that I would try to paint a watercolor, I opened the box and read the note again. Looking down, I saw that a layer of mildew had grown over every single pad of color, so that there in my hands was a uniform field of gray. Well, so it goes. It was absurd and yet so appropriate that I started laughing, which was the beginning of my coming around.

It would be hard for me to say what I accomplished in Sierra Leone. It would be hard, too, to say what I learned that I have used in the rest of my life since then. I remember one night sitting up with some African friends talking about tribalism and belonging. One young man, a high school student named Sam, was a Sherbo but was living with us in Pujehun, which was mostly Mende territory. He made it clear that he lived in Sierra Leone, but he considered himself a Sherbo first, and a Sierra Leonean second. When I talked about American citizenship, I tried to explain how any person born on American soil immediately becomes an American citizen. This was too much for him. He argued that you are who you are because of who your parents were, and the tribe they were a part of became your tribe, regardless of any accident of birthplace. He could see it no other way. I had always assumed Americans were sure that being born in the USA made one an American, but Sam could not be convinced of the wisdom of that stand. It seems that some of our leaders are not convinced of it today.

I learned that in Africa a white skin opened all doors, but not very far. I have not kept up with any of the Africans I met in those two years, and that may be asking too much of the work friendships we developed. We were friendly, but never friends. Inequality in relationships makes friendship hard. Once in the last few weeks of our time in Pujehun, I was invited to a reception at the district council. Some Big Man was visiting our town and the district officer was hosting a party to welcome him. I was flattered to be invited and was enjoying myself and the scotch being generously poured. After a couple of hours, I realized that I was the only white person in the room, and that was just fine.

A few months later, when I was getting off the El returning to the seminary on the South Side of Chicago, I realized I was the only white person there on the street, and it was definitely not just fine. I was probably more afraid than I needed to be, but I was certainly more afraid that I had ever been in West Africa, except maybe when we were on leave in Nigeria taking the train north, and waiting for morning light to cross the Niger River, which was rumored to have bombs planted on the bridge. Within a couple of years, Nigeria erupted in the tribal slaughter that unfortunately has become the fate of so much of Africa during the past 30 years. But that's another story. I remember conversations with other volunteers about the happy prospects for Sierra Leone. We were told, and believed, that this little part of the British Empire would benefit from British influence and remain stable as a two-party democracy and grow prosperous as the nation learned to extract and use its mineral wealth. Sometimes these things work out. Maybe it will now.

We were young and naïve and more than occasionally rude. I am embarrassed to remember how many times we sang "We gotta get out of this place, if it's the last thing we ever do" much too loudly and too late at night. Our neighbors were unfailingly polite and gracious to us in spite of our boorish ways. Someone once said that the problem with PCVs was that we were smart but not wise. Perhaps the wisdom of Africa came to us only through living an African experience, and remembering it years later.

# 2.

# Life Lessons in Pujehun

*Richard Pflugfelder*

My Peace Corps service was truly a watershed event in my life. The greatest lesson I took home from Sierra Leone was a clear understanding of the difference between a standard of living and a quality of life.

I grew up in a functional, loving middle-middle-class family, comfortable, secure and a little sheltered. In retrospect, a little less comfort, security and sheltering would have better prepared me for Sierra Leone and my life beyond. I have always been intrigued by people with a gift for happiness that doesn't depend on how many cars or bathrooms they own. In Sierra Leone, I was amazed to find people whose grinding poverty, by American standards, seemed to be no obstacle to happiness and a rich quality of life.

Africans often exhibit a kind of nobility and spirituality that I find very appealing. Those traits were prominent in a Mende man called Pa Blackie, who became a friend and mentor to me. He was uneducated but wise and highly respected in his village. He was able to devise practical and compassionate solutions to problems and resolve the conflicts that were often the source of the problems. Ingenuity and human capital must often substitute for financial capital in Africa, and Pa Blackie was a master at mobilizing them. I had the feeling that Pa Blackie understood things about life that I might never learn. People like him make a huge difference in every community.

Another person I remember vividly was a woman named Jeneba, who lived next door to me in Zimmi, the headquarters town of Makpele Chiefdom, in the Pujehun District. She had two children and a husband working elsewhere who wasn't home very often. A recent TV movie entitled *The Magic of Ordinary Days* made me think of Jeneba. She had an amazing gift for finding joy living in the present and doing ordinary things. Her smile and persistent cheerfulness were contagious, despite the challenges of her life. Watching her animated conversation and laughter while pounding rice with her friends, one might have thought she was lounging in a hot tub with a cocktail instead of doing menial labor. The image of Jeneba is often there when I see Americans suffering from "affluenza."

My Peace Corps experiences and life lessons continued in Vietnam in 1969–70. I was drafted and went through Army training and deployment to Vietnam with a strong instinct that it would turn out OK, and it did. The night before my infantry company was sent to a forward base camp, my Peace Corps service got me assigned to a Civic Action unit. Do you remember the wartime expression "winning the hearts and minds?" We worked with a tribe of Montagnards called the Jarai, closely related to the Hmong. They lived in tidy, functional villages with individual family compounds. Despite surviving for millennia, they were deemed to need more security. Four nearby villages were forcibly moved to a new consolidated village, laid out in rows and columns, affording little privacy. My first months were spent dismantling bamboo houses and moving unhappy people and their belongings to a place they didn't wish to be.

The Jarai were among the gentlest, happiest people I've ever known. Living among them, I learned how much close-knit families and communities can contribute to a high quality of life. Their laughter and joy of life flowed as freely and purely as the water from the abundant local springs. Learning to speak their simple, alliterative language helped me appreciate their way of life even more. We built a school for them, and provided some medical care and market trips, which helped to compensate for their forced relocation. My year living among the Jarai, instead of combat in Vietnam, counts as one of the luckiest breaks of my life.

Forty-five years later, the world is a very different place, and I am a better person for those experiences. I'd like to think that the grandchildren of the people I knew can still achieve a high quality of life without much material wealth.

# 3.

# The Coatses' Legendary Peace Corps Experience

*Bill and Barbara Coats*

W e joined the Peace Corps due to Barbara's enthusiastic response to JFK's call to national service. To paraphrase our assassinated president's words, she asked not what her country could do for her but what she could do for our country. Barbara was going, whether or not I agreed to go; this became a condition of our marriage. I was more cynical, believing that the motives of our government went way beyond peace. I thought of this "New Frontier" mission as more like the old frontier, when white men first went out and made friends with the Indians, or, as we say in the 21$^{st}$ century, "to win hearts and minds." I was motivated to apply not only for my love for Barbara but in reaction to a draft board physical I had been compelled to take. Deferrals were then granted married men, and the Peace Corps seemed a better alternative than going alone to Canada.

We worked at one thing or another through high school and college on jobs that included waiting on tables, cooking, cleaning, factory work, recreation therapy in a state mental hospital, as well as farm and construction labor. We had worked with disadvantaged youth from New York City in a New Jersey camp during the summer of our marriage, 1964. Our politics and experience in civil rights demonstrations contributed to our desire to further contribute to the betterment of oppressed peoples. Although neither of us had shown a talent for learning other languages, we were nonetheless accepted as a couple to train for a rural and agricultural development project in West Africa. We had never before left the country, traveled west of the Mississippi or south of the Ohio, or flown in an airplane.

# Training

During the early days of training at Hampton Institute, Barbara realized that a young western woman, without children, who was neither a teacher nor a nurse attached to an educational or a health service program, was going to have a difficult time launching development projects in a rural community. She developed a "let's wait and see what happens" attitude and was determined to enjoy herself. Meanwhile I became enamored with the idea of becoming a builder. My construction skills were being recognized by the staff and other volunteers. I started to foresee opportunities to build things like schools, clinics, roads, bridges, wells while helping host nationals to build their institutions.

Meanwhile, we were having a great time meeting, having long animated discussions, and drinking with other volunteers from across the country, from different backgrounds but all with a common passion for doing good works. Our conversations were about our short life stories and self-promoting polemics on all the vitally important topics of the day. Having our training conducted on the campus of a black college seemed to heighten the intensity of our discussions related to the civil rights movement. Some volunteers had been freedom riders in Mississippi and had marched on Washington; others were present as their schools were integrated. Many of us felt we were part of a great wave that could alter the balance of opportunity between the advantaged and disadvantaged. There was also skepticism. We were obsessively concerned about who among us were CIA or FBI plants, and who was most likely to be "de-selected" for expressing or having associated with others holding extreme political views. We dreaded the psychological and sociological tests we took as instruments for determining our fitness to serve.

We questioned the appropriateness of training when we made a trip to a massive pig packing plant and when we were taught farming techniques that were right for Virginia but not applicable to the tropics. When Isaac Schaver was told to illustrate how to plant a palm tree, he struggled to break the impervious Virginia clay with a pick that weighed almost as much as he did. Asked what he thought he could achieve if he couldn't even plant a palm tree, he replied, "Dispel the myth of white superiority." That I believe we achieved. We loved our "host country nationals" and liked some of the returned volunteer trainers. We went to the bar in town where we listened to "Louie Louie" on the jukebox, played shuffleboard, and drank copious quantities of alcohol. It was rumored that there were some of us who were smoking marijuana. It was during a party for the de-selected volunteers that I first was exposed to the weed that had become more prevalent by the time we returned.

Our second training site was in the small town of Profit, on St. Croix in the U.S. Virgin Islands, a tropical paradise with green hills, white sands, and deep blue waters. Some of us were assigned to stay in a newly constructed low-rise public housing project. The view from our work site was beautiful, with sugar mill ruins, palm trees, and the Caribbean Sea visible from our hilltop worksite. We spent long days in the hot sun building a cinderblock recreation center, and long cool nights eating and drinking with other volunteer couples. We deepened our attachments, which were further nurtured during our stay in Sierra Leone.

## Sierra Leone

Flying in an old twin engine plane with Russian pilots, we got our first sight of the startling red earth, deep green foliage, and massive clouds over Freetown. The city seemed somehow familiar because the tin roofs looked like those in a Caribbean town. We were introduced to departing volunteers, CARE officials, and Star beer before we were sent off toward our posts. Most postings were not in places where the languages we had struggled to learn were spoken. Barbara and I were told that we had been specifically chosen for Kagbari, the headquarters town of a chiefdom in the Bombali District. It was in a remote area, with great health and safety risks, where a guesthouse was to be built, which we were to occupy for our stay. When we got to Makeni, the district capital, we were hot, tired, and glad to be in the Peace Corps rest house, until we started talking with volunteers who were waiting to leave. They sang "We've got to get out of this place" over and over and said how miserable they had been and how misguided the idea was that couples would fare better. They boasted about having recommended Kagbari as a joke, which the naive CARE staff had taken seriously.

It turned out that we were to live on the porch of the alcoholic chief. The house sat on a slight hill overlooking 10 or so thatch-and-wattle houses on both sides of the road that ended in front of the chief's house. We had two small rooms at opposite ends of the porch, one serving as a kitchen and the other our bedroom. For the most part we lived outdoors, on display for all the curious folk who had seen very few if any *pumway*, white people. Due to the presence of cattle, there were flies that we only escaped while under our nets in the bedroom.

The CARE staff told us that the chief had agreed to supply workers to help build the guesthouse, but not a soul ever showed up to work.
I drew a floor plan, started making blocks, bought lumber, nails, and
cement and started a foundation. No one paid attention to the drunken
chief, and no one was willing to work if not paid. We were stubborn and
refused to continue working on projects that were not supported by the
local people, holding to the idea that we were there to teach and help,
not to be the new paymasters. But work did not progress. We were
physically sick much of the time, were sick of being on display, and we
were increasingly sick of each other. We decided that we would ask for
a transfer, and if that wasn't granted, we would leave the country.

Our transfer approval came on a rare day when we were thinking
things might work out in Kagbari. We had become attached to some of
the children and had come to anticipate and love our visits from Bob
Galeria, who had a truck and was stationed in Samaia, farther north in
Bombali, nearer Guinea. He was welcome company and assured that
we were supplied with beer and other essentials. Yet we believed that
our enduring for the full term or with each other was at risk if we stayed
in Kagbari.

The opportunity to move came about because our friends Cathy
and Jim Harmeling suddenly decided to quit and go home. We moved
south to the Pujehun District, almost the whole way across Sierra
Leone, to the town where they had been posted, Blama-Massaquoi, the
headquarters of the Gallinas-Perri Chiefdom. There we were provided
with a well-furnished cement house with six rooms, five cannibalized
"Made in China" bikes, a latrine, a water filtering system, a houseboy
named Moybay, a dog named SuSu, and a petrol refrigerator. It was a
far cry from living on the porch in the north. Soon after we arrived we
made friends with a 12-year-old boy named Momodu. Moybay, the
houseboy who had been hired by Jim and Cathy Harmeling and whom
we were expected to retain, got water at the village tank and washed and
ironed our clothes. We developed patterns in our days that included
lying on our hammock on the porch with SuSu, reading, with coffee in
the morning, tea in the afternoon, and Johnny Walker Red or Star beer
in the evening. We took long walks or biked with our young friend
Momodu or Francis, the court bailiff.

Our lack of meaningful relationships with Africans and failed
development projects furthered our sense of alienation. It became easier to stay in our village, where at least we had the pleasure of reading
volumes from the two book lockers we had acquired at Kagbari and
Blama. We looked forward to the next lorry, to see who had come or

what might be aboard. Wayne Walthers and John Root, Peace Corps volunteers who were also posted in Pujehun District, were welcome visitors with whom we drank, talked, and played cards. Well, they were not always welcome, because the maddest Barbara ever got with Wayne was when be brought a third person, in addition to John, thus having ruined our plans to play bridge. Our greatest in-country pleasure came when Gretchen and Steve Bingham came for a wonderful and extended Christmas visit. Another great time was when John and Ann Cole came to stay for a couple of weeks. We reciprocated visits to their places. Other than these visits and seeing a few others with whom we were close, we soon got tired of volunteer and expatriate gatherings in the rest-houses and clubs in Bo and Freetown, where it was not helpful to hear the constant complaining by others no less depressed than ourselves.

For a time just after we arrived in Blama, the chief appointed me as his driver of his black Humber, a British-made car that no one else knew how to drive. We made day trips with a case of Guinness stout between the driver's seat and the back where the chief sat fully robed and happy. We paid visits to his WWII British African Corps buddies, in police stations, court *barres* and porches. They openly spoke in English of their war experiences, their wonderment at such as the Leopard Society, the prevalence of woman damage (young men having to pay for having had relationships with other men's wives) and their disdain for politicians who sought power through the purchase of human internal body organs. One night the chief asked if I wanted to see spirits that he could see lurking around me and others, but he insisted that I must admit to what he had shown me. I said I would have to think about that. After consideration, while sober the next day, I told him that I would not, because I would then worry that back home I would be thought psychotic and put in a mental hospital. Another night, after we had stolen a Boy Scout toy telegraph key from his friend the police chief at Kenema, at about 2 a.m., his first wife came to our door to ask me to come and talk with the chief about his keeping everyone awake. I found him tapping out Morse code messages into the night on the battery-run key.

"Chief," I said, "To whom do you think you are sending messages?"

"Oh, no one really; in the North African desert I was sent encrypted messages that I could not read and sent them on to the British, who I never saw. I enjoyed doing it then, and I am having fun doing it now."

All the travels stopped after a couple months when the car broke down and the chief found that his Peace Corps driver could not, or as he suspected would not, fix his Humber. The relationship, for all intents and purposes, ended at that point.

We could observe, all too easily and with a few questions, that no one had solid bowel movements. Water contamination was most likely a factor. The first project attempt was to dig wells in villages where there were leaders who said that they had a water problem and the desire and ability to deliver the labor necessary to resolve the issue. I had put together one workable bicycle from the parts of the other four Chinese-made bicycles that CARE had supplied for those of us whom they somehow determined did not need a truck or motor scooter. With energy boosted by cola nuts, I rode five to 15 miles each way to villages across the chiefdom's length and breadth. After a couple months of visiting about 15 villages three or more times, I had found nine that agreed to work with me to put in wells. I ordered nine hand pumps from USAID, but after months of waiting, only two pumps got to Blama. I was informed that the balance of the order had been diverted by the district officer in Pujehun. I picked a village that seemed most excited by the prospect of having a well, offered the best chicken chop, and happened to be less than five miles away. I read a book on how to determine where best to drill a well. I explained to a gathering of older men about our not wanting the well too near the river, to avoid contamination, but not so far as to disturb the socialization of the women and children as they gathered to load buckets and carry water back to the village. I asked where they wanted their well.

One man excitedly told me where it should go as he pointed and said, "This is where the last Englishman put a well."

I could see an indentation in the ground and asked, "Why hadn't anyone told me?"

"Mr. Bill, you came to build wells, no?"

"Why was it abandoned?"

"The well was poisoned by enemies."

I asked, "So, enemies poisoned the well. What? Germs, people from another village, or spirits?"

They spoke between themselves for a bit before Francis interpreted, "It could have been any of those reasons. They don't know."

I asked my final question, "Do you think that such a poisoning could happen again with a new well?"

"Oh yes it could, Mr. Bill, it certainly could."

I sent the two pumps to the district officer in Pujehun the next day.

There are so many other tales I could share illustrating our collective Peace Corps presumptions and our collective personal ignorance. We ordered 10 bags of a new rice variety, called Anathota, which had been developed in-country for planting as an upland or swamp crop. I got one bag; the balance had been diverted, just as the pumps were. We were instructed how to show farmers the robustness of Anathota by setting up a four-square demonstration to compare the new variety with their seeds and to show how chemical fertilizer could increase production. An old farmer interrupted me as I was measuring for a demonstration plot. He asked to be given a handful of the new seeds. He bit a grain, tasted it and told me to wait, he would be right back. He brought out rolls of cash, saying that he would buy all I could deliver. He explained to me, and others agreed after examining the seeds, that they know rice very well and could tell that this was a fine variety.

In another instance, we ordered a prefabricated school to replace the dilapidated grass-roofed classroom, but we never learned what happened to the new materials. Further illustrating our collective ignorance, we planted temperate-zone seeds given to us through CARE so that these tropical farmers might learn how to garden.

The Current Judge, known to us as Al Haji, was a dignified and gentle man who had made the pilgrimage to Mecca. We became acquainted during his stays in a room off the porch of the house where we lived. We had developed a mutually respectful relationship, due in large measure to his dignity and excellent English. When he saw the rice bag arrive on the porch and learned about the project and how planting in paddies increased yields, he wanted to try this new variety and plant Anathota in a low field we could dam near his village. He wanted to overcome the annual shortage that resulted in "hunger times." This project was completed as planned; workers showed up daily, worked hard, and understood the potential gains and risks involved. Yes, higher yields could chase away hunger, but one could also contract schistosomiasis while working with bare feet in standing water, planting seedlings in the paddies created by damming the creek. By this time CARE had granted me a motorbike, another benefit obtained due to a volunteer leaving the country. I had boots that we shared as much as possible and loved working with the men day after day during those last few months. The Al Haji proved to be a kind and resolute leader of his village and of our work. Forming a bond of trust proved to be essential to the work being accomplished. We heard later, from a volunteer who extended his stay, that the yields had been bountiful and that they had created a surplus. Our hope was that with some money they could buy the rubber boots needed to reduce the health risks.

While on leave traveling across West Africa, we resolved to stay in Blama upon our return. As a result, we came to find joy in many long days watching our neighbors carry water, build fires, cook, make music, dance, *palaver*, and from time to time weave country cloth in long five-inch-wide strips stretched around and between the buildings. We watched the old men gather in the court *barre* to talk and doze off during the hot dry-season days and observed the women bring their children when the health clinics were held. We saw and participated in the burning, clearing, planting and harvesting of rice and cassava. We loved when the traders came to unfurl their wondrous goods before us, from huge bundles carried on their heads and backs. The rolling thunder and sheet lighting during the rainy season was astounding. We saw rice dried on the ground, winnowed, and then pounded into the whitest of flour by strong women, often with babies on their backs. Woman would bring their babies to show us. We never knew quite why, but they were beautiful. Troupes of dancing devils arrived with flag boys and musicians drew all the people in the village out of their houses and into the gathering crowds. We came to appreciate the smiling faces and the extraordinary courteousness of the people. Yet we never felt that we really understood their thinking, nor did they seem to understand ours. With the exception of Francis the bailiff, Momodu, and the Al Haji, we formed little more than superficial attachments.

While in Freetown on a trip made necessary by an attack of dengue fever, we purchased fireworks from an Indian merchant, anticipating a celebration of our Independence Day with our neighbors during our last month in-country. Near the court *barre* there was a patch of sand surrounded with boulders that looked like the best place the set up the 20 or so rockets and other items. Once it was dark and a crowd had gathered, I lit the first fuse. But these were not the kind I had purchased in Ohio when I was 15. These were the real thing, used by professionals. The first rocket was so hot that it set off all the others in rapid succession. Explosions, blinding flares, and rockets zoomed high into the night sky and over the thatched roofs and beyond. The crowd gasped and shouted in amazement. We were petrified that we would burn the whole town down. All went off in less than 30 seconds. We were all in a state of wonderment, and after we realized that there were no fires, we joined in the uncontrollable laughter. We left the village a few weeks later.

Before we could leave, the district officer and his wife invited us to visit at their home. As we had tea and chatted, he asked how our families at home had been during our long absence. He wondered how we felt about leaving them for such a long period of time without being there to watch after them, while in Africa attempting to help strangers. He found it hard to understand. He said that he had heard that I was upset by his having diverted some of the pumps and rice. I said that yes, I had been angry and felt that it was a kind of theft. He said that he wanted me to understand that he took them for his people, the Mende, who had been captured, enslaved, and sold to the English by the Massaquoi, a clan of the Vai tribe, with whom we had been working. He thought it fair to take a portion of the goods proportionate to the Pujehun District population distribution. He went on to say that he had been supported by his family in his pursuit of an education that included attending Oxford, in England, and that he owed them his efforts to ensure that they received a fair share of resources available to the district.

We had known about the Massaquoi role in the slave trade. They had shown us with pride the silver scepter Queen Victoria awarded them for their contribution to the empire. We had hiked 18 miles to the slave port where the tip of the Gallinas-Perri Chiefdom meets a protected inlet of the sea. We spent an eerie night in a tent next to a huge cannon, surrounded by holding pens, with steel chains with cuffs, not far from stairs that led to where captive people had been loaded into rowboats and taken to ships just off the coast, bound for the West Indies. I simply had denied to myself the obvious historical connections that would influence the relationships among these peoples. When we got back to Chicago, the same patterns were glaringly obvious, in that benefits were distributed and flowed to the families, and ethnic and racial groups (tribes and clans) to whom those in power owed their allegiance. I was embarrassed for myself, the Peace Corps, CARE, and USAID for our collective ignorance.

We cried as we boarded our last lorry out of Blama. We would miss our dog SuSu, who somehow knew we were leaving; she would not come out from under our bed as we packed. We would miss Momodu, with whom we had formed a deep bond. Otherwise there were no goodbyes. We did not see the chief, the speaker, the judge, or the bailiff, though we had been told months before that there would be a big send-off celebration. We felt there was a mutual feeling that it was time for us to leave, and the less said the better.

## Back Home

We arrived home after traveling in Europe for a couple months, thinking that family and friends would have a great interest in our experience, but with the exception of Bill's mother, there was very little. After the first few, our slides were no more interesting to them than their baby pictures and vacation slides were to us. It was obvious to us and some new friends that we had had a transformative experience. We knew that we would never understand people from other cultures beyond a superficial level, and we no longer could take our own culture for granted. The two-year odyssey has continued to influence our social work careers, personal relationships, and aesthetics. What we read and watch, how we travel, and how we decorate our home have been shaped by our West African experiences. We have handled the myriad crises in our lives since 1967 differently from how we would have had we not experienced and survived those two years together.

As Paul Simon sings, "Still crazy after all these years."

# 4.

# Life in Shenge

*Susie Getzschman*

Even today when it pops up in daydreams, I am almost as physically repulsed by the images drawn by Eugene Burdick and William Lederer in their book *The Ugly American* as I was when I read it as a high school junior. My disgust for a picture of the United States filled with self-centered, arrogant, and culturally insensitive people coalesced within me, forming a vague plan to major in political science and minor in languages, initially French, in the hope of joining our country's diplomatic corps after college. But as with so many things, this secondary-school vision morphed through my college years into a fine arts major with an English minor and political science and French courses to pad my CV.

Then JFK exploded onto the national scene with something he called the Peace Corps, which solidified my dreams of being useful to other cultures into a two-year commitment to live and work in a third-world country, in order to prove that Americans loved other cultures and wanted to know them intimately. So as a college junior I applied to join that idealistic organization.

Meanwhile, I began spending my free time with a student librarian, Bill, a son of the American Great Plains, who threatened to spend all his days in Omaha, Nebraska. I told him of my firm post-college plans, and he said little, just listening to me with a dreamy look in his gigantic hazel eyes. When I asked to borrow his car to drive to St. Louis to take the required government test for Peace Corps service, he said, "No need. I'm taking the test myself." He had applied, as well. Eventually, we married.

Our raucous, seemingly endless training lasted from August to December 1965, during which nearly all eighty-nine of us in training argued acrimoniously, in multiple forums, for personal viewpoints backed by a wealth of ignorance. Just after Christmas and Ramadan, we took off for Sierra Leone via Dakar, with Harmattan winds from the Sahara covering everything in a fine layer of sand. Bill and I clung to the least of expectations, but we were assigned to Shenge, the principal town of the Kagboro Chiefdom, in Moyamba District, a tropical paradise overlooking the Atlantic, framed by picture postcard palms and gilt sunsets. Bob Golding, who managed the CARE contract from the Peace Corps that ran our group, confided that he knew he had a perfect fit to direct the building of the outboard motor repair shop that had been requested by Shenge Chief Madame Honoria Bailor-Caulker. He had read in Bill's resume that Bill had built a kayak! We stared at him open-mouthed. Given that Bill had built it for himself from a kit and that kayaks are propelled by a paddle, our confidence in the process was shaken even before we arrived at our village and discovered that not one local boat that could accommodate a motor safely.

Our lovely chief, the democratically elected illegitimate daughter of the previous chief, couldn't wait to meet us and present her cherished agenda for Bill. She wanted Shenge, population roughly 489, to be a Mecca for American tourists. What did Bill think of building a shopping center on the main street of town? We would have to kill most of the sore and parasite-infested dogs slinking around every round house, but that was easily done. Bill politely suggested he needed time to settle in and evaluate what projects he felt he could take on before diving in. But Madame would have to wait until our boat was repaired, and we and our Peace Corps predecessor, Ed Clinch, motored from Freetown across the bay to Shenge before those sensitive negotiations could begin.

We slid the boat into the water in Freetown on a windy afternoon, and we discovered only after we rounded the Freetown peninsula that the wind had grown to a gale, blowing right at us from the south. By nightfall, we had made it only about halfway in what Ed swore was normally a two-hour put-put. "No problem!" he bellowed above the engine, "We'll just drop anchor and take off after dawn." So in our small scow, loaded with six months' food supply and very hard board seats, we cut the engine, dropped anchor, and pretended to sleep. We gloried in the thickness of the Milky Way in a moonless tropical sky and the clarity of the constellations, not that any of us could even begin to navigate by them.

Just before dawn we woke without a speck of land showing anywhere! "Sh—! The bay must've been too deep for our anchor cable!" Ed set about cranking the engine ferociously, which seemed suddenly loath to turn over. He cranked and cranked until Bill suggested he just let it sit for a minute as we "prayed like 60." It finally began to catch, on maybe the hundredth try, which made us wonder, "So how do we know where land is?" and "How much gas do we have left?"

Suddenly we were blinded by an enormous spotlight. Ed speculated that it was an oil tanker, as they often hugged the coast of Africa in their journey to supply Europe and the United States. Ed decided to steer between what he thought would be the coast, to our left, and the ship, to our right. Within a half hour, we spotted Monkey and Plantain Islands, just off the Shenge coastline. Bill would later dig foundations for a new primary school at Plantain Island.

The crowds on the Shenge beach stared as the new *Potos* docked. The beach was awash in people as several fishermen had just arrived back, and people were dickering for *bonga*, small fish, to smoke and sell. We learned that the beach served as the local latrine, its water table so high that fresh water ran down the beach at high tide and helped to wash away the day's waste. It didn't make us hanker to swim there, but it did alleviate the usual foul odor of the alternative latrine, the bush.

Ruth Clinch, Ed's wife, ran down the bank to meet us, and we were immediately swept up in a happy local crowd. I couldn't avoid noticing that I was the only woman there without holes in her ears and not built much like the local ladies, including Ruth. I was asked if I was old enough to be married, at age 22. When school let out, we met the local Peace Corps teacher from the primary school, Kathy Hufnagel, a rangy, broad-shouldered woman of perhaps 5' 11" with humor-filled, close-together blue eyes, freckled nose, very fair skin, and corn silk blond hair sporting remnants of a year-old perm. My new neighbors all declared in loud terms that they would never be able to tell us apart; we looked identical. I begged to differ, since I am 5'6", with straight, long, thick, dark brown hair and brown eyes and tannish skin. But it was an amusing echo of a problem some people had at Hampton Institute, as we effectively integrated the school during our training.

Ironically, that boat would never function again. We discovered that it should *never* have worked because someone had neglected to install a key part in Freetown, and there were no available Mercury engine parts to be found in West Africa at that time. It was declared a miracle that we had gotten out of Freetown at all in that boat and utterly impossible that the engine had started out in the Atlantic. And it was totally out of gas when we arrived. Apparently we had motored in on fumes.

When we had been formally introduced, and the Clinches had departed by lorry for Freetown to complete their term by manning the Peace Corps hostel, we settled into our new home. It was a white-washed CINVA ram block home with corrugated metal roof, resting atop a tiny cliff between the ferry dock and the local mosque. We bought the Clinches' bottled gas stove, set up our water filter so that we would have some drinking water, and moved in our supplies, including lots of ketchup, a Getzschman staple. Blown away by the presence of our own refrigerator, albeit a kerosene one, I didn't yet have anything to freeze, but I chilled the milk we reconstituted from Dutch powdered tinned milk, which required heated water to turn it into decent drink-able stuff. I also chilled our limes, lemons, and oranges bought from the crowds of sellers bearing them on their heads. I couldn't locate any tomatoes or onions, so we wrote home for seeds, hoping to find some locally sooner.

Although we had been warned against "culture shock," neither of us seemed afflicted with it except that I battled the apparently endless varieties of insect colonies that wandered in and out of our house at will. My first sewing project was to join our two mosquito nets together so that we could push the single beds together, but occasionally I still awoke from dreams of fire ants marching up the sides of the bed.

Snakes loomed large in our first lessons about Shenge. Alpha Brima, our across-the-street neighbor, grocer and mosque crier, served as our snake expert. Whenever we spotted one, we asked him if it was one of the 38 deadly poisonous varieties or one of the seven harmless ones. Alpha always assured us that it was one of the deadly ones, per-haps just to keep us on our toes. But one afternoon, we found one about which there was no doubt.

We had taken a lunch break on our porch facing the ocean, which was beyond the strip of bush that Bill had fashioned into a small banana plantation with all the varieties we could find. Bill suddenly jumped up, ran to the edge of the bluff, and motioned to me. A small crowd of neighbors chased a wriggling line down the beach toward the scrub brush behind our house, shrieking and throwing sticks, shells, and rocks. Bill raced for our storage area to grab a rake, a shovel, and an umbrella. As my mouth formed a question, he yelled, "Watch me!" and ran down the sandy ferry-landing road to the beach.

Leaning over the bluff and holding my breath, I recognized the size, color and markings of a black spitting cobra rising up before Bill, spreading its hood and extending its fangs. Holding the open umbrella with his left hand to avoid the blinding venom, he slammed the rake over the back of the cobra's head, pinning it to the sand. As the snake lashed to free itself, Bill sliced at an angle with his spade, severing head from body in a single strike. Wild cheers and dancing erupted from our neighbors as they picked up the still undulating body of the cobra and held it over their heads. Those deadly fangs lay on the beach, the black head outlined against the white sand.

Several more snake scares served to explain the serious warning our friends gave us with regard to collecting flora for our yard. Bill had taken plant taxonomy in college, and I'd grown up with a love of flowering plants and trees, so we had planted some gorgeous fireball lilies from the bush to add to our view and thought we might continue collecting. We had also hoped to plant some sort of grass in the "yard" to clean up the endless mud that covered the earth in the rainy season. When our neighbors saw what we were up to, they asked if these were good for food. "No, they're just beautiful," we tried to say, discovering there was no good word for aesthetic things in Krio or in the Temne language we had learned in training. When we came back with grasses, they put their collective feet down and told us that the flat area covered in dirt that extended 20 feet in all directions from the house protected us from dangerous snakes. Not more than a day later, I found a small snake in the storeroom attached to the house and ran to get Alpha. He proclaimed it, "Very bad, Missus!" But it disappeared under the lumber before I could get Bill to work his magic. By that time, he had begun work on the famous outboard motor repair shop for which he had been selected. After that, we abandoned all horticultural plans except for the banana plantations, one at the Evangelical United mission grounds and the one behind the house, and we left the mud alone. However, Bill still planned an irrigated upland rice experiment for the dry season.

Bill had his work cut out for him, traveling to the village of Kata and to Plantain Island, looking at building schools in our own village of Shenge, and jousting with our chief over her "shopping center" plans. He also discovered the previous year's project overseen by a Moyamba Peace Corps volunteer in an earlier group. The chief had convinced her people that they needed a brand new jetty to tie up all the cruise and other tourist boats that would soon be flocking to Shenge, so she mustered all her communal labor muscle and Peace Corps smarts and spent a year building a nice concrete jetty out into the bay. The day we first saw the project, low tide exposed its folly: the jetty was mired in mud and sand that stretched at least half a mile farther out into the bay.

Nothing larger than a flat-bottomed scow would ever land there, even at high tide, and precious few scows ever were employed for tourist transport. The worst part was that the concept of communal labor was dead in the water; no one had benefited from this project.

Bill managed to find enough of the oldest children at the school to put up the frame of the new secondary school, but the man assigned to be his second-in-command never materialized. The only worker he could absolutely depend upon was a dear, toothless old Temne man who introduced himself to us as Pa Molai. He performed an excessively polite morning greeting each day, and we could hear him coming, talking to himself and chanting, "*Kong, kong, kong kong, Undirai, Missus!*" to which I replied, "*Sekay, yo!*" This he followed with, "*Yo, sekay!*" and so on and on. It was evident that he couldn't find work as a Temne in a Sherbro area influenced by the Mendes, totally dominated by the Krio and Mende languages. He showed up at 6 a.m. daily and politely asked Bill if he had any work. He worked hard every day, and by the time we left, he was able to actually buy a shirt and shorts in one piece, in which we had never before seen him. The only thing that saved his modesty was that holes seemed to be in places that didn't matter and cloth barely covered what clothes were intended to. He wore only rags to work and took off his shirt when he worked in order to "save" it.

The first construction project was building a big exemplary chicken hutch of bush sticks and palm fronds, with a grass roof, all of which was tied together with vines, so that no one would have to pay anything for materials should anyone decide to put one up. We added a little trough of hollowed out bamboo to give the chicks water to drink and included the husks of rice with a few grains of rice for food. Then we bought some local chickens and a couple of Rhode Island reds, and we were soon awash in fresh eggs. Our neighbors never asked how we got all the eggs; they let their chickens run free, so finding eggs was difficult and eating chicken legs was like eating solid rubber. We had plump, not muscular, chickens to eat when they quit laying.

The coop was a raging success. Even the chief heard right away about our chickens and had a coop constructed for her household. Of course, hers had to be built of concrete block with a zinc pan roof. Since she refused to give her chicks water or rice, within a couple of weeks she had fried chickens in her fancy coop. She said that clearly such coops didn't work. When it was suggested that she'd have to feed and water the hens since she no longer allowed them to scratch for their own food or find water, she strenuously objected that she'd never had to do such things before. What an absurd expectation! The local dispenser also found it annoying to have to water them, but he eventually capitulated when he saw the prolific eggs our hens laid.

Since Bill gathered quite a crowd in building his coop, he decided it was a great time to give the official "Peace Corps volunteer" speech. We didn't yet know he was speaking Temne to mostly Mende and Sherbro speakers. So he launched into, *"Un gwament gna do Amerika somra su noi."*

Within a minute a man was tugging on my shirt saying, "Please, Missus, ask de man to talk English." Bill cracked up and spoke with a man, who seemed especially attentive to what Bill was doing under the Petromax lantern. He had been instructing his children in how hard Americans work compared with the British, and he offered to translate into Sherbro or Krio. Pa Julius Caulker Brown had been an especially effective teacher who was enormously popular in the village. Since the chief's husband was Minister of Education, Mme. Honoria was able to have Brown transferred up north to Makeni, using the excuse that he had married a Temne wife and would fit in better there. As a member of the loyal opposition, he knew she just wanted to get rid of him, so he refused to go and lost his job. He then became a progressive farmer who worked well with Bill, but he came down in his social status by no longer being a teacher.

Brown couldn't afford to work for Bill on any of his construction projects. Only Molai showed up to begin on the famous outboard motor repair shop. Bill was almost at a loss as to what to do when one of the local police wives showed up to ask for work. The wives said they had been particularly frustrated recently because when the policemen were off duty, instead of helping around the house, they simply spent their not-so-hard-earned salary on palm wine rather than fish or rice or something for the women to cook and feed the children. These women had taken their sorrows to the chief to arbitrate, who sympathized, also being a woman. She suggested that they apply for any new jobs that might come up with the Peace Corps man. Then their lazy husbands could have no say as to what might be done with the money.

Bill was pleasantly surprised to have 20 women working with him, gathering volcanic rock in their head pans and getting paid by the pan. A few men came by later and agreed to help them crush the rock and make CINVA ram blocks before they began construction. Soon, it was a going concern with old Pa Molai as the second-in-command. The women came faithfully, and so Bill created a local social revolution in Shenge with the wives of policemen earning more than some of their husbands.

With that project humming along, Bill thought he would try doing something he had seen in the *Village Technology Manual*: building a windmill that could pump water up from the high water table. While we had water pumped up manually into a tower to flow down to the bathroom to flush the toilet, sand inevitably worked its way into the pump, making it more and more difficult to pump the water up to the tower. So Bill thought that the prevailing winds from the west off the Atlantic would power the mill. Sadly, he never found all the parts, and though the windmill turned and made noise, it never did the job for which it was intended. If it had, it would have revolutionized Shenge. The mill was just another nighttime job Bill did while other men played with their children or wives, or, if the moon was full, celebrated the ancestors and danced until dawn. Bill settled for setting up a small stove underneath a gallon drum to heat hot water for our makeshift shower.

During the daytime, Bill worked on agricultural projects or on the motor repair building. Later at night, he wrote a record of his activities in a journal so he would remember what he had done in the time he was abroad. Between the school foundations and planning, the motor repair building, and his "inventions," he really accomplished a great deal in his short year in Shenge.

On the other hand, it was tough being married to this phenomenon, since as soon as the women found out I was not a nurse, as Ruth Clinch had been, they lost all use for me as a leader. I strung up a line for my washing, rather than draping it around on the ground, hoping to lure some women into following suit, but only a couple did, when they found it helped cut down on the Tumba flies, which laid eggs in the clothes. The larva burrowed under the wearer's skin for sustenance, causing large open sores.

I started an infant feeding program, for which only a couple of women turned up. They became my best friends. Naomi Sumner was my closest friend. Her children all bore different last names. Her husband, teacher Sumner, had left town in shame after she could bear him no children. Almost immediately thereafter, she became pregnant with the first of many children, proving that she was not the unfruitful partner. She faithfully named the children for their various biological fathers. She used the CARE milk that I was trying to sell the mothers on, rather than the fatty custards that made babies look fat but gave them almost no nutrition. Naomi told me all the gossip that no one else would tell the white woman. I got to know her children on a personal basis, as I did the Muslim children of the wives of Alpha, the grocer across the street.

We loved having the children running in and out of our home. Little Brima was the boldest. He always wore a shirt but often no pants. He took very seriously his job of carrying water on his head from the public well twice daily. His sister Isatu didn't take to us right away. I used to chase Bill around with a frying pan for their entertainment. They roared with laughter and begged for more. When Bill realized they had no toys, he made them a rocking horse, which they didn't understand how to use. Bill had to get on it and ride screaming "Me na cowboy, na cowboy!" Then they got the idea and occasionally they came over and used it, but mostly those bush sticks with a coconut head and shells for eyes just sat forlornly in our yard. I don't think the father approved. It flew in the face of his very strong work ethic. But he made the kids attend when I set up a small preschool in the living room. We taught songs and little poems in English, and I know those children did well in school later.

I gradually took over the work of the agricultural officer. Bill was so busy with the building projects and with the other agricultural projects that he had no time for seed dispersal or to show folks how to plant things or how to use them in cooking. I enjoyed listening to the people getting off the ferry and seeing our gigantic Burpee tomatoes, "Oya! Na tomatis? NO! Oya! Na beeg, beeg one!" Then a few minutes later, I'd hear the soft knock at the door and, "Missus, me na get one seed, one-one seed?" Then I'd sell them one small packet of seeds for ten cents, a huge investment for them but which they valued because they paid for it. Afterward I would show them how deeply to plant, how closely to watch them, how to water and prune the vines and how I used them for cooking.

We had a visit from the local *tiefman*, too. One afternoon Bill was strolling up the road toward the village of Tisanna, where Pa Brown's farm was, when he spotted a man wearing a shirt with our college name on it. That sounds innocuous enough, but when the college you went to had only 600 students and lay 5,000 miles away and served a religious denomination no one in Shenge at that time had ever heard of, and you had worn that very shirt to work only a couple of weeks earlier, Bill stopped him and asked where he had found the shirt. "I buy it." The man said truculently, not giving ground to the tall skinny white man. "Hey, those are my swimming trunks you've got on under your shorts!" Its distinctive waistband showed above his low-slung pants.

By this time a large crowd had gathered as this promised to be pretty good entertainment. Imagine a white man catching the hated *tiefman* red-handed! Any kind of palaver was high entertainment for the town residents. In the end, the accused promised to go into a house and remove the clothes.

"Missus, ee go ot de bak, looky!" cried a neighbor, and sure enough, the house he found had a back door, and the thief was flying out across the mini swamp in the center of town. The crowd wanted to follow him and carry on the row, but Bill had already headed home, so the chase petered out. We did find out that he had hooked our laundry bag from the bathroom window that was never closed. We had moved the next bag because a row of tiny ants had found it a good place for a nest, which made me a little (sorry) antsy.

Our Shenge days were generally happy, sunny ones, but I couldn't get Bill to take a vacation. I wanted to see Nigeria and Cameroon, which would have interfered with his upland rice experiment in the dry season, so we had to remain at home. I was so disappointed that I took off alone in a lorry headed for Bo. I had an idea of visiting Ed and Judy Griggs, who were stationed up near Makeni, but I never made it that far. I started the trip at 4 a.m. in the rear of an industrial-sized lorry with the other travelers when they left Shenge for points north. The driver, a big, well-built man, forced me to move up front, where he proceeded to make me a lewd offer. I had been warned how to handle such a situation, so I put my fists on my hips and furiously told him that I had a "Great big man and he go beat you!"

The driver had done his mandatory duty, and I had done mine, so he roared with laughter and we got along famously for the rest of the trip. Actually he talked my arm off, and I learned a lot about the life of a career "cowboy" who spent his time on the road, and he protected me from other opportunists hoping to get rich off an ignorant American woman. I visited Maria Martin and Janet Nash, our group's volunteer women in Bo. They had no idea what to do with me, so I went back home, lonesome for Bill. Our disagreement about travel was the only serious argument we had as a newly married couple on our first assignment abroad. Later, Bill went home to heal an ulcerated cut he got on the job, and I was left alone in Shenge for a month.

Other Volunteers in our group came down to visit, as they'd heard that we had lovely white sand beaches and two banana plantations and good cooking. I think maybe the two farm boys from upstate New York, Roger Thompson and Ted Keefe, were out of cash, and since Bill and I had no obvious expensive bad habits, we had plenty of food and could be sponged off. The two Bobs, Galeria and Baggett, came from points north. I was grateful to have the company, and Bill was happy to have me looked after. And that's how our service terminated.

After being informed that Bill was going to stay in the States in order to heal the ulcer, I traveled to Freetown with our trunks (subsequently lost at sea) and checked out for departure by air with Dick Shira. Dick was terminating out of loneliness, I think, since Frances Nolting, his placement partner, had quit and gone home to Paris. We traveled via Marseilles and Paris, where we debarked and visited Frances in her family's lovely pension on Avenue Foch. We visited many of the Picasso retrospectives around town and L'Opera, and then I finally departed for Washington, DC, and home.

While we may not have fulfilled all our aspirations, I do think that we definitely changed the people of Shenge's view of Americans from being rich, unapproachable people, to friends unafraid of hard manual labor and willing to do what we could to offer them possible ways to a better life. Along the way, we inadvertently witnessed social change and small evolution in the thought about agriculture and chickens and views about cow's milk. Meanwhile, we gained an invaluable perspective on what the United States looks like from a third world county. Now I think that living in a third world country should be mandatory for U.S. citizens before they are permitted to vote in the U.S.

# 5.
## Life and Death in Sembehun

*John and Betty Wuesthoff*

Ｗe awoke with a start. Though it was only 4:30 in the morning, people were wailing outside our bedroom window. I jumped up and ran to the window, meeting only darkness. The voices came in a haunting and melodic rhythm rising from the town directly below, up over steep, craggy cliffs to the building in which we slept. Arabic was the language, and prayer to Allah its theme. We heard the prayer five times a day during our stay in Sembehun, yet it never lost its fascinating novelty.

The building in which we slept was a dormitory at Fourah Bay College, the "Athens of West Africa" as it has been called, a college with an elite student body of 300. Our first impression on arriving in Sierra Leone was that we had disembarked somewhere in Asia. Not far from the airport we ferried across the bay to Freetown, the capital city. We were suddenly surrounded by picturesque "Chinese junks" with a crimson sunset as a backdrop. On coming closer, however, we saw that the faces of the Asians on the junks were black and the language they spoke, Krio, was an African Creole English. The junks were African fishing boats, indistinguishable to us from their oriental counterparts.

We left Fourah Bay College after a four-day stay and traveled up-country by Jeep and Land Rover, over some of the worst roads in the world, to meet the chiefs with whom we were to work. Most of the chiefs we met spoke excellent English and were quite pleasant. They were the chief administrators of their chiefdoms and so were quite powerful.

In Moyamba, the following day, we met the head of the Moyamba District. The district contained more than a dozen chiefdoms and was headed by a district officer, who was more powerful than the chiefs. In fact, they were often in awe of him. Our district officer, a handsome man of about 35, well dressed and obviously self-confident, came out to meet us. He smiled often and spoke to us in fluent English. "Abdul Karrim," he gave as his name. He, his police guard, interpreter, chauffeur, and Betty and I squeezed into his Land Rover and drove over a potted red dirt road 18 miles to our village, Sembehun, the headquarters of Bagruna Chiefdom.

When we arrived in Sembehun, Mr. Karrim strutted with a Truman-like briskness to the courthouse. We trailed along behind him. Once in the courthouse, a long concrete building with a zinc roof, we were met by 70 townspeople waiting patiently for the show to get under way.

"Mr. and Mrs. Wuesthoff are here to help you help yourselves," said the district officer to the assembly. I doubt the significance of this phrase was understood by the audience. "Would you care to say a few words?" District Officer Karrim asked me. My few well-practiced words were, "*Nya gohu nengo bi lova.*" Which, literally translated from Mende, meant, "My belly fills with sweetness when I make your acquaintance."

We were the first "Europeans" they had heard speak Mende, and the assembly burst into laughter. Our success was, we thought, assured.

## Breaking the fast

The last Sunday of January marked the end of Ramadan, the Islamic "Lent." We were dressing for church on that Sunday when a young boy appeared at the door carrying a golden-brown, freshly roasted chicken smothered in onions and spiced with red hot peppers, which he had brought from the chief. A note the boy held invited us to eat the chicken, visit their service, and so share the breaking of the Ramadan fast.

With ecumenical spirit we walked some distance toward where we heard the now familiar prayers. Three hundred beautifully robed Muslims were gathered under three gigantic cottonwood trees and were sitting cross-legged upon woven straw mats.

We were late and vainly tried to remain inconspicuous as we sat at the rear of the gathering. Only the women sit at the rear of such an assembly. We were able to see over all the heads and noticed our paramount chief in the front center, dressed in pontifical white robes, his tall frame topped off by an equally immaculate, though not quite pontifical, fez. On his right and left sat all the headmen of the villages within his chiefdom. The chief turned and beckoned to me [John].

I walked around the assembly toward the front, leaving Betty behind. All prayer ceased as I threaded my way through the periphery of the brilliantly dressed crowd. There was silence except for the hundreds of yellow songbirds nesting in the cottonwoods. I'm an incurable romantic, and exhilaration overcame me as I sat next to the chief and quickly removed my shoes, as is their custom. The praying resumed. An hour later, the service ended. The chief rose and called Betty to him. "Please walk with me," he whispered to us.

Throughout the village streets we walked at the head of a parade, the chief taking great pains to protect us from the scorching sun by holding his massive rainbow-colored umbrella over our heads. Two drummer boys walked ahead of us, beating a rhythm to which the women chanted more Islamic prayers in Arabic.

The hour-long parade ended at the chief's compound, where Betty was seated on his left and I on his right, as he greeted all the visitors from the surrounding towns, occasionally dropping a shilling or two into an eager palm. That evening the chief gave each of us a native tie-dye garment, an attractive gown for Betty and a fancy shirt for me, both made from colorful local hand-woven cloth.

The day had been exhausting, and we were happy to return to our dwelling, where we shared an uneasy relationship with a small family of bats.

## Devils, friendly or otherwise

Devils may not be any more numerous in Sierra Leone than in America, though they are certainly more visible in Africa. The prime minister visited Moyamba, our district capital, and we had an opportunity to see him and meet some devils. Drums and cymbals were booming and crashing day and night in our village for several days preceding the visit. Many people, including the devils, practiced their rhythms in anticipation of dancing for the prime minister.

"Many devils will be there to see the prime minister," a friend said to us, "and I'll introduce you to them." "Don't worry," he said, "They are friendly devils; there are no bad devils in this district." We met several of the friendliest devils in the world that day.

On another day, a Friday afternoon, we were walking down a sunny Moyamba street lined with mud-block houses. In the distance men were chanting mournfully. Suddenly, three middle-aged Africans came running toward us, yelling hysterically. "The devil, the devil, the devil is coming. Seek shelter or you are doomed!" One of the men grabbed me by the arm and I grabbed Betty and the five of us raced toward one of the crowded block houses. Up on the veranda we ran. "No! No! This is not secure," cried one of our escorts frantically, as we raced to the next house. Our pounding on the door brought an old man in T-shirt and short pants to open it. "The devil is coming. These people must hide!" Our escorts quickly departed as the old man secured the door and hastened to cover himself with less revealing trousers. He limped toward his closed wooden shuttered window to hazard a peek. His face paled and he quaked in fear at what he saw. "May I look?" I asked. "Oh, no!" he replied. "Should the devil see you you'd be dragged into the bush." "What then?" I asked. "Oh," he said, "Terrible things."

We remained with the old man until he assured us the devil had disappeared and we could safely venture outside. "The devil is no more," said our host.

We had been at least partial participants in the Poro secret society initiation, a men's society with its roots in old tribal wars and designed to train young warriors to vanquish their foes.

## Bringing in the groundnuts

Gardening in Sierra Leone is often disappointing but always enlightening. Farming techniques there have changed little in hundreds of years. The crudest of implements are used, and modern techniques are difficult to introduce. Those who are farmers typically have seven plots, each covering an acre or two. Every year a man chooses one of his plots to farm so that in a period of seven years he has completed the cycle and is back to the first plot. This seven-year fallow system for each plot is thought to give the soil time to restore its minerals. The rate of bush growth in seven years is fantastic, and every year, as the farmer changes from plot to plot, he encounters a huge forest which he must cut and burn.

We tried to introduce crop rotation and fertilizers to restore soil minerals and thus avoid the long fallow period, reduce the burden of land clearing, and increase the amount of land under cultivation at one time.

Superstition and custom play a large part in farming. Because of the land scarcity, we decided it would be a good example to grow a crop on land available to most everyone: the front yard.

The opposition we encountered surprised us.

"Europeans put flowers in their front yards. It is no place for crops," Paul, our Sierra Leonean friend, told us.

I replied, "But you're always talking about your lack of good farm land. Your front yard has good soil. Why not use what is available?"

"Front yards are for flowers," he replied.

"Can you eat flowers?" I asked.

"No!" he answered laughing.

"Then we're not going to plant them."

"All right," he responded, "But no crop will grow there."

We decided to plant peanuts, known locally as "groundnuts," a crop containing a high level of protein, a nutrient that the native diet sorely lacked. The villagers told us that our front yard had too few rocks to grow peanuts successfully. We asked them what a rock gave to help a peanut grow. This they couldn't tell us, though they were convinced that rocks were a necessity.

We raked the ground and removed all the rocks. They all shook their heads. "Crazy Europeans," they must have thought.

With the assistance of commercial fertilizers, the peanuts grew vigorously. People stopped to tell us how surprised they were that the nuts were growing so fine without rocks. The peanuts caught the attention of a friend who was a *juju man* who advised us that *tiefmen* would take the crop if he didn't protect them with his juju. Consequently, the next morning we found a coke bottle tied to a stick that had been driven into the ground, and inside the bottle were written juju notes which did, indeed, have the intended effect.

With the aid of our friend who had wanted the flowers in the yard, we harvested the peanuts two months after planting, two to three weeks earlier than everyone else. My friend was counting the number of nuts per plant. "How many?" I asked.

"Fifty," he answered happily.

"Is that good?" I queried anxiously.

"It's wonderful! The most we ever get is 15 or 20."

"Paul," I said excitedly, "Tell your people about this! Tell them I used no rocks but plenty of fertilizer."

"No!" he said emphatically, "They will never believe you grew so many and all the villagers will call me a liar."

## A child's death and baptism

Although death occurs frequently in Sierra Leone, it is as sorrowful as anywhere in the world. There is weeping and wailing and all-night vigils the two nights following death. On the seventh and thirtieth days, there are ceremonies similar to an Irish wake.

Once, we were watching a woman behind our house straighten the hair of a five-year-old girl whom we often met drawing water at the well adjacent to our residence. The straightening is done by heating a large fork-like instrument and running it repeatedly through the hair. It makes the hair "like a European's."

A couple of days later, we heard that the little girl was suffering from the Africans' most common killer, malaria, and she died a day or two after that. We joined the Roman Catholic schoolchildren kneeling in the dirt outside her house to say the rosary. We then visited the house, as is the custom, and viewed the dead child. "The girl will be buried today," a friend told us. "Had it been a boy, perhaps tomorrow. Boys last longer than girls."

Her body was carried to a lorry where women held it while relatives of the child argued with the driver over the price of carrying her corpse to the burial ground. "One Leone 70," said the driver.

"One Leone 40," responded the dead girl's uncle.

"One Leone 50," said the driver.

"OK," said the uncle.

The wife of the Catholic school's headmaster, Ma Ma Fefegula, was crying because the child had been taking instructions in preparation for baptism but had never received it. "It's too late now," she said to me.

"There is no agreement on the part of Catholic theologians as to what time the soul is said to leave the body of the deceased," I said to Ma Ma Fefegula. Why can't I baptize the child? I thought.

As though reading my mind Ma Ma Fefegula cried, "Oh, please, please do it."

I ran to stop the lorry as it was starting down the road. It came to a halt. "There's a Christian theological viewpoint," I began explaining to the gathered mourners. They stared blankly at me. "Oh, never mind. I'm going to baptize the child." I called to Betty to bring me a cup of water.    "Wait, how long will it take?" the driver asked me.

"What's that have to do with it?" I thought.

I jumped into the lorry and removed the blanket covering the child and tried to remember the words and formalities of baptism I had learned years ago. The mourners watched closely, listening intently as the European drove away the evil spirits with his water medicine, strange words, and hand gestures. I then covered the child, and the lorry, overflowing with grieving relatives, squeaked down the dusty, blood-red dirt road, on its way to cross the river and climb the hill to the local burying ground.

# 6.

# Life, Black Magic, and Death in Telu

*Barry H. Hill*

## Sex for Water

The Mende tribe is a matriarchal society, and although men often (but not always) perform the heavy labor, most all the decisions in households are made by the women.

The village of Telu, where I was posted, is the headquarters of the Jaiama-Bongor Chiefdom, located near Bo, the capital of the Bo District, in the center of Sierra Leone. The area was characterized by heavy swampland. It was hot and humid, and water was in great demand by the people. In my village, all the water had to be carried from an area of relatively clean swamp water about three-fourths of a mile from the center of town. All this water was carried in buckets on the heads of the women. Given the heat, the humidity, and the distance to be carried, to say that getting enough water for a family was a burden is a big understatement.

My wife Carol and I had been living in Telu for about six months when, one afternoon, talking with the paramount chief while we swung in big hammocks on his large front porch, the subject of potable water came up. I'd noted to the chief that the amount of effort and burden just obtaining water for the people to drink and cook with was awful to contemplate, let alone getting minimal amounts of water for bathing and washing in the nearly unbearable heat and humidity. The chief gave me his characteristic "Harrumph," meaning that he was about to come up with an idea or two. He said, "Let's go to my warehouse." We walked the couple of hundred yards to this building and the chief led me to a remote back room. Opening the door, he gestured toward a couple of hand water pumps and a large pile of 1½ inch pipe, as well as pipe-threading equipment and various pipe connectors. He then related that a Dutch aid organization had donated the pumps and equipment about five years previously to selected chiefdoms for trial. But, he said, there had been no instruction or assistance provided to actually install pumps on wells to see if they worked. I asked him to give me a couple of weeks or so and we might come up with an idea for making use of the equipment.

I returned home and broke out my handy Peace Corps handbook on assisting folks in rural areas. The table of contents revealed a section on simple wells with hand pumps. Everything looked simple enough, at least in a first reading. The following weekend, I was due to travel to Bo for my monthly R&R, which would be spent at the Peace Corps volunteer rest house, where there were a couple of Peace Corps engineers I could consult, and I could also talk with our local CARE–Peace Corps project leader, who might have some sources for help.

Sure enough, engineer Charlie Dent was full of information about wells with hand pumps, since he had been raised on a small farm in upstate New York where hand pumps were still used for potable water. He filled me with all the information that my neophyte brain could absorb. It looked feasible. I returned to Telu on Monday with some encouraging words for the paramount chief. I sketched out a plan to experiment with the pumps and parts he had available to install a well just outside his compound where he could keep a close eye on its use so that we could assess whether additional work might be worthwhile. He agreed, and rapidly we formed a small new project for wells. He then provided me a chiefdom-funded counterpart, Momoh, who would serve as the project manager.

We developed a schedule for a start-up. The chiefdom would use its funds to buy the cement to construct the well platform, pump base, and access door, bolts for the pump installation, and other miscellaneous parts. The chiefdom would also pay for the services of the shallow well digger, who was put to work digging the well the next day. I was also able to get a message via a traveler going to Bo to talk engineer Charlie into coming out in his Jeep pickup to help us for a couple of days.

The fateful day arrived. Everyone assembled around the already-dug well, which was approximately three feet wide by 20 feet deep. We numbered about 10 altogether to do the work of constructing the well platform. We made a small framework for holding the concrete in place, mixed up the stuff, and poured it in, being careful to use another frame for the access door and also carefully placing and installing the bolts to hold the pump in place. We finished the work in the early afternoon and departed for our homes, allowing the well platform to cure in place.

During the entire platform pouring process, there were no fewer than a hundred women in a circle around the men, watching very closely. The next day even more women, nearly all carrying buckets, arrived to observe the work.

The next morning all of us gathered around the well platform. First we tried wooden levers to attempt to pry the well platform into place. That didn't work. It was simply too heavy. Charlie noted that this problem might be the reason that simple wells hadn't been dug and pumps hadn't been installed. However, counterpart Momoh came up with the solution. "Let's do this the African way," he suggested. "We'll lift it into place." I was never ever able to figure out the exact weight of the platform, but a near guess might be 1,500 to 1,700 pounds. Six of us gathered around the platform, and in response to Momoh's shout to "Heave!" we gave a mighty lifting motion to the platform. Nothing happened. No movement. It was too heavy. Momoh then said, "Wait." He went door to door and came back with six more men to help. Lining them shoulder to shoulder around the platform, Momoh shouted, "Heave!" once more. Groaning, the 12 volunteers moved the platform about six inches. "Again!" Momoh shouted and the dozen heaved once more. It moved nearly a foot this time. After three more tries, the platform was finally placed in position over the well. Brute strength and numbers had conquered gravity. We then fitted the pipe to the pump, bolted it in place, and Momoh was given the honor of making the first thrusts of the pump handle. We held our breath. Hurrah!! Suddenly water spurted from the pump, and my heart began beating again. Momoh invited one of the women to fill her bucket with the clean water. A queue then formed immediately with the other women carrying buckets, and all took turns pumping the handle, but the water was pumped dry after about the twentieth woman had filled her bucket. It would take a while for the well to refill after such heavy usage.

As I later learned, many women gathered around the well throughout that first night, patiently waiting for the well to refill to accommodate the demand for the clean water. Momoh faithfully stood on duty to monitor the well, and the chief was also frequently present to monitor the pumping.

On the morning of the third day, we gathered in the chief's compound for a meeting to assess where we stood. All present pronounced the program viable and potentially operational. The chief advised that he would bring the program's potential to the Chiefdom Development Committee meeting the following week. Meanwhile, he also authorized the installation of a second well, this time about 50 yards from my house, where I could also monitor the program. That well was installed about a week later, and we then had two wells to observe to try to determine viability of the project.

The acceptance of the two wells and use by the women was beyond expectations. Momoh questioned them periodically to ask why they liked the well water, and the overwhelming response was that they did not have to walk a nearly two-mile round trip to get the water, closely followed by the observation that the water was "clean."

On my next monthly trip to Bo for R&R, I told Charlie the engineer and my CARE leader about the success of the water well trials. Both were very encouraging. Charlie advised that he had recently been to Freetown and had visited a U.S. Agency for International Development (USAID) warehouse where he had spied what he estimated to be about 150 water hand pumps with associated pipe, pipe threading, connecting parts, and other miscellaneous equipment. Charlie also gave me the name of the USAID staffer who had taken him to the warehouse. I was due to travel to Freetown for a routine physical exam (our Peace Corps doctor was very solicitous of our health) so I determined to contact this USAID fellow to see if he might share the resources of his warehouse with my chiefdom.

The USAID guy was very encouraging, telling me that as far as he could determine, the water pumps and equipment had been untouched in the warehouse for over 10 years. He said he would contact headquarters to see if he could get permission to release the equipment to the Peace Corps.

A month passed, then six weeks, with no word about the pumps. I thought, hey, my Peace Corps tour is only two years, and time is burning through my timetable. Then suddenly the USAID rep appeared at my door. He was on his way to the northern part of the country and had detoured through my chiefdom to "give me the news." Evidently, there had been a row between USAID and the Peace Corps over some small slight, and USAID headquarters had advised the rep not to release the equipment to us. He'd tried in vain to reason with them, he said, but they were unrelenting in their view. Then, he advised that the pumps and equipment were just taking up space needed for other material, especially bags of food aid, and that he would welcome getting rid of all of it. He then told me that on a certain prearranged date, I would be able to back up a lorry to the door of the warehouse on a late evening and somehow find all of that equipment located at the doorway ready to be taken off. About a month later, we used Sierra Leone-style "midnight auto supply" to obtain those pumps and equipment, and the paramount chief's ware-house was the sudden recipient of nearly a ton and a half of simple water well pumps and equipment.

Boy, were the women excited. The news spread like wildfire throughout the chiefdom that the water well equipment had arrived. Momoh, my counterpart, reported receiving delegation after delegation of women from villages throughout the chiefdom, asking to be included in the well program. He and the paramount chief had started a list of villages eligible for participation in the program. The require-ments were that the interested village had to come up with sufficient funds to provide for the salary of the well digger, the cement, the wood frames, the bolts, and other miscellaneous gear required for the instal-lation. The pumps, pipe, pipe threading equipment, and other small gear were provided through the program.

Everything went exceedingly well and beyond our expectations. The list of requests for wells kept increasing, and we found that over 30 small villages had come up with the funds required and were asking to be scheduled for installation. Conferring with the paramount chief, Momoh and I figured that to meet the demand we needed at least four more installation teams to be formed, trained, and fielded. Village women were sending delegates to the paramount chief daily, pleading to obtain early listing on the installation schedule.

The teams were able to install about one water well each week in each participating village from that point on.

Then, disaster struck. Three or four of the previously installed wells experienced pump failure. Picture women dejectedly leaving the site of a well with the buckets unfilled, requiring a long walk to the swamp. Evidently, the leather packing around the pump housing, used to seal off the pump shaft to create a vacuum, had failed. There were no spares provided in the USAID- sourced equipment. What were we going to do? Then Momoh again suggested, "Let's do it the African way."

Momoh then contacted the local "handyman" in Telu and showed him the problem. It's truly hard to believe how fast this entrepreneur found a solution. Evidently, there was a local vegetative plant that exhibited "sealing" characteristics in its fiber similar to that of the leather pump seals. The handyman installed this fiber patch on the first failed pump and immediately found success. The pump worked per-fectly. In fact, the Peace Corps staff found that after the program had spread to other chiefdoms, a new business had been created in provid-ing seals for the pumps, as well as seals for other uses and needs.

After about six or seven months into the well-development program, Momoh found out that there were two villages that had been trying unsuccessfully to gather the funds necessary for participation. The women in these villages had tried to no avail to persuade their men to cough up the funds necessary to meet the program's requirements. These villages were known for their men's palm wine production and drinking. Weeks went by, and the women continued to report no progress to the paramount chief in getting their men to provide the funds for installation of the wells.

More weeks went by, and still there was no word on finding money for the well installations. Then one day Momoh appeared at my door, announcing that representative women from the two villages had suddenly appeared in the chief's compound with the cash required for the well installation. Momoh claimed that he did not know the reason why the women had finally been successful in obtaining the funds. Rapidly the wells for the two villages were installed. Only much later did I find out through the grapevine that the women in the two villages had gone on sexual strike until the men coughed up the money required.

After the Peace Corps, I eventually ended up working in agriculture and natural resource development for USAID. Along about 1985, the agency suddenly came out with a "new" policy that began emphasizing working with women in the development process, whereas previously the concentration had been only on males. I personally found this strange since I had begun working with women almost exclusively while serving in Sierra Leone in 1966–67. Much, much later in my career with USAID, I found similar results from such sexual tactics in other regions of Africa. Today, no one discounts the influence and direction that women have in Africa over the development process.

## The Leopard People

Nearly every morning I awoke in Telu after a night having dreamed of events that had occurred the day before that were truly astounding, in my experience. One of the more incredible events that I experienced in the Peace Corps involved the Leopard People. This was near the start of a career that included many years working on international development in Africa.

Upon arriving for Peace Corps service in Telu, I first met with the paramount chief, who sat me down in his second hammock on his front porch from where he instructed me, over the next year and a half, in how I might best conduct myself in helping the chiefdom. In fact I'd been instructed by Peace Corps, through various sources, to listen closely to my local African sources for hints as to how I'd best be able to conduct myself so as to best benefit the people.

We were terribly under-trained, badly indoctrinated, inexperienced, and ready to help anyone in the general concept of "community development," the name used to describe our activities. Between agriculture and school and road construction we had been peripherally trained for many different trades, but suffice it to say, we were clearly the master of none. We were, rather, prepared to assume the job of facilitator. As a group, we were fresh out of college or were coming from a farming background, but we had no practical overseas experience whatsoever. We were set, by inexperience alone, to learn from our aid recipients many times more than we'd ever be able to contribute in return, a fact that the Peace Corps readily acknowledges.

When I arrived in Telu, the paramount chief, in his initial hours of introduction to the chiefdom, told me that he had placed *juju* bags at strategic locations at the corner roof points of my house in order to exclude the devils that might try to invade. My first reaction to this instruction was, "Of course there were not any devils. It's all superstition, right?" But that is not so, as I later learned, to my ultimate benefit. And bless the paramount chief for what he did.

Eight months later, the benefits of the chief's advice appeared. One morning just before sunrise, I awoke to a cacophony of drums. The noise of the drums was astounding, almost capable of damaging hearing. Even today, I cannot recall the noise of those drums without some sympathetic pain in the depths of my ear canals. My God! It was an unbelievable volume. And, as I recalled later, the sound was not without rhythm. There was a syncopation to the drumming which became clearer as the morning dawned.

Jumping out of bed, I ran to the living room windows and looked out to see a large circle of costumed men surrounding my house. Looking closer, I was able to see that they were all wearing the skins and preserved heads of leopards. Each had a small drum at his waist and danced in rhythm to the drumming. Running to the back windows, I quickly determined that the circle surrounded the entire house. I later estimated the number of them to be about 50–75. Then I saw my pet chimpanzee in his small enclosure around a tree in the back yard screaming and gesticulating wildly, scared by the noise.

At this point, the houseboy came into the house, telling me to keep my head down and to step away from the windows. He then ran to the doors to check the locks, while moving to the windows to close the shutters. He cautioned me in a loud voice to not leave the house and stay inside. I told him that we needed to get the chimp inside. He immediately shouted, "No!" At this point I became sufficiently awake to become scared. "My God," I said to myself, "What is this?"

Meanwhile the noise of the drums increased in volume and cadence, and looking through the cracks in a window shutter, I noticed that the dancing pace had also increased. Suddenly a portion of the circle of men broke ranks and feinted toward the house, bringing them to about 20 feet away, but then they immediately moved backward and rejoined their circle. The sound of the drums increased again, and the dancing pace grew accordingly. I found myself shaking with a combination of curiosity, dread, and fear, but mostly fear. The paramount chief had warned me about the Leopard People when I first arrived. Now this warning was being played out in my front and back yards. "My God," I said to myself, "What have I gotten myself into, coming out here to Africa?"

The minutes and hours passed. Around about 8 a.m., I heard a loud cry from outside: "Barry, are you hearing me?" I cracked open a window shutter and spied the paramount chief standing outside the circle in front of the house. I shouted back that I heard him. "Listen carefully," he said. "Do not leave the house under any circumstances and follow my instructions to the letter. Do you understand me?"

I replied, "Yes!"

"I'm going to return in about an hour," said the chief. "Meanwhile, stay in the house and don't leave for any reason."

I acknowledged his instruction and closed and relocked the window.

Then came an emergency! I heard the chimpanzee scream so loudly that I could almost experience his pain, and I ran to the back window. A phalanx from the circle of leopard people had collapsed inward, to form up around the chimp's tree, and they were working through the door to remove him from the cage. He was jumping all about, trying to avoid their grasping hands. Then my houseboy, who was very attached to the chimp, bravely ran out to the enclosure, shoved aside his leopard opponents, grabbed the chimp and ran to the house, bringing him inside. Safe at last! The chimp grabbed onto my chest, as usual, then wrapped his hands and legs around me, digging his nails closely into my back for security. He was safe!

Never in my life did an hour move by so slowly. Finally the clock wound slowly past 9:30 a.m. The drums of my leopard-clad circulators remained steady, strong, and very loud, but then I began to hear another beat of drums. Opening a front window shutter, I was able to see a large group of people coming down the road. At the head, I could see the paramount chief, followed closely by a medicine man at least nine feet tall, in a hideous costume with a horned multi-colored head and strings of what seemed like blood-colored saliva dripping from his mouth. This group, led by the paramount chief, moved up to the circle of leopard-clad people and stopped. The drums of the leopard people ceased. Then the 25 or 30 drums of the paramount chief started in their stead, followed by a steady shout of words from the medicine man. As the minutes passed, the line of leopard folk began to break, making off into the bush at both sides of my house. After what must have been at least an hour, I discovered that the circle of leopard people had departed my house entirely.

I invited the paramount chief inside my house, leaving the medicine man outside. The chief reminded me of our conversation regarding *juju* when I'd first arrived in the chiefdom. He said that what had "saved me" were the four *juju* bags he had hung from the four corners of my house. He said, "Rest, and we'll talk further about this incident."

About two weeks later, I visited the chief and asked for clarification of the incident: "What was I saved from?"

He looked down at his feet, then to the ceiling, then at me, saying, "The Leopard People issued a proclamation last month saying that if a leopard group were able to obtain a white man's heart, that would then give them an extraordinary amount of power to confront their enemies. And even further, if that heart were to be combined with the heart of a chimpanzee associated with the white man, the power would be doubled."

I trembled inwardly. "My God," I asked myself, "Had we come that close?" I then asked for clarification, only to find him reluctant to explain. The only thing I could get from him was that "further explanation would only be available in the Mende secret society." But I never joined the Mende secret society.

## Witch doctor curses kill children

Life was hard and disease rampant in Jaiama-Bongor Chiefdom. Living among the rural people gave Carol and me the opportunity to carefully watch and observe how precarious the lives of our new friends were. Disease was rampant: elephantiasis, malaria, blackwater fever, dengue fever, and awful skin diseases, especially among the children who had serious open sores on their lower legs, were among another dozen tropical diseases, both waterborne and airborne.

Early on, we learned that local people dealt with the trauma of early deaths among their children in a unique and somewhat sad fashion. Simply put, they believed that their children "belonged to God" until they were five years old, when, finally, they could be considered to be their own. After living among them for a year, we were able to estimate that indeed, over 80 percent of the children died before reaching the age of five. And we finally had to admit, and believe, that one of the chief contributing factors to such early deaths was witchcraft. This is the tale of one of those children's passing attributable to *juju* and witchcraft.

Asate was the 10-year-old daughter of my neighbors, 50 feet north of our house in Telu, the chiefdom headquarters town, in Bo District. Asate had been the first town resident to welcome us into our new house upon our arrival. Smiling, gracious, and seemingly wise beyond her years, she was a delightful child. And as the weeks and months of our residency passed, we became ever closer to her.

One of Asate's favorite pastimes was joining me on our front porch after the workday was over around 5 p.m. I had hung two locally made hammocks from the roof-beams and Asate swung herself into one while I occupied the other. The first item on our agenda was always language learning. She had taken it on herself to ensure that I became more and more capable in the local Mende dialect, and in turn, I had promised to practice English with her. We'd spend a useful half an hour at this effort when, at that point, I'd call the houseboy and ask him to bring Asate a glass of juice. We always kept fresh-squeezed juice from whatever currently harvested fruit we could obtain in our kerosene-fueled refrigerator. Asate always expressed wonder about how cold it was, since she had never in her life enjoyed a cold drink. She gulped the liquid down rapidly so she could then ask for more, which we always quickly provided. Then she'd pry herself from the hammock and go on home. Never did she overstay her welcome, and she seemed to know instinctively when I was hot and tired and needed to get to the bath shed at the back of the house.

Asate and I became closer and closer as our volunteer days passed in Telu. We began to ask her to share meals with us. She also delighted in playing with our pet infant chimpanzee, and we watched the two of them become better and better friends. The pet parrot also became one of Asate's best friends, especially when she brought some nuts and leftover maize porridge to share with him.

We had lived in Telu for about a year when, one afternoon, Asate didn't show up. I waited about half an hour for her and then walked to her house next door. Pa Bende, her father, opened the door and I immediately noticed that his eyes were blood red and his voice was shaking. I inquired about Asate, and he ushered me into the house and took me to her room. She lay on the bed without movement of any kind, her breath labored and uneven. In my faltering Mende, I tried to ask him what was wrong, but his reply was spoken very quickly, and I didn't fully understand what was wrong. He mentioned something about a witch doctor (or witch doctors) that I could interpret, but the remainder was completely unintelligible to me.

Alarmed, and very worried, I hurried down the road to the paramount chief's compound and luckily found him at home. I explained the problem with Asate and asked if he could accompany me to her house to help me find out what was wrong. The chief then invited me to his front porch where we sat in his hammock, as he said he had something to explain to me. He started by saying that what he was about to reveal involved matters of the secret society, so he was very limited in what he could discuss. Then he asked me to keep what he was about to say strictly between us.

"There's nothing physically or medically wrong with the girl," he confided. "Her father got into a terrific argument and shouting match with the town bully, a man whom I knew of. The bully contacted one of the witchdoctors and asked him to place a curse on Pa Bende's child. As you can see, she is paralyzed. Within a week she will die. There is absolutely nothing any of us can do." I reared back, shocked beyond belief and not accepting what he was saying. The paramount chief then said that he could say nothing more about the situation and that I was just going to have to accept this fate for her.

Of course, my Western reaction was immediate and brusque. "Chief, I just cannot believe that. Who would put a curse on a child?" I complained. "No way! No way! I'm going to take her to a doctor." The chief grabbed my left forearm and forcefully made me sit back in the hammock. "You have to accept this. Curses are most often made upon the children of people in disputes with each other. Just think. If you had such a disagreement with someone, whom would you rather have cursed, him or his child?" Immediately the point shot home, and I understood the rationale. Still, I just could not bring myself to believe that such a thing could be done. After all, this was the 20th century, not the dark ages, when the occult was common. Then I asked the chief again to accompany me to Pa Bende's house to see Asate. He reluctantly agreed, and we walked down the road together in silence.

Upon reaching Asate's room, the chief went to her bed. He beckoned me closer and told me to take her hand. The little appendage hung limp in my fingers. The chief went to her head and pulled up one of her eyelids. The iris was rolled back, leaving only the white of her eye exposed. He told me this showed how extreme her condition was; her brain was shutting down and nothing could be done.

I told him that I still wanted to take her to a doctor. Expressing frustration, the chief told me there was nothing anyone in modern medicine could do. The curse was of the permanent kind, which could not be lifted by anybody or under any circumstances, he assured me. He took me by the arm and led me out of the house. I went home next door, and Carol and I talked into the early hours of the next morning. I decided that I was going to take her to a doctor.

I took the houseboy next door to Pa Bende's house and explained to him and his wife what I wanted to do. Both of them, even in the depths of their sorrow, immediately tried to convince me that the trip would be futile. I kept insisting and finally after an hour, they told me they would concur. I asked Pa Bende if he or his wife could accompany me, and he agreed that she would go.

About six months previously, we had attended a Peace Corps twice-yearly meeting at the site of a Catholic missionary hospital run by Irish nuns, three of whom were doctors. The hospital was about a hundred miles from Bo town, a whole day's journey by local lorry. The next morning, I was able to stop one of the local lorry drivers and ask if I could charter his truck to take Asate to the hospital. He agreed, and Asate, her mother, and I climbed into the lorry late in the morning.

Just as the sun was descending below the horizon, we arrived at the hospital. I picked up Asate, who lay limp in my arms and uttering no sound, and we began walking toward the hospital. Her mother walked quietly behind me. As we neared the entrance, one of the Irish nuns, whom I'd met during our meeting, opened the door and came out to meet us. Her first words were, "You know there's nothing you can do about the child. She will die." Astounded, I immediately demanded how she knew that, as she had not even touched the girl. "I've been here a long time, my friend," she replied. "I've seen hundreds of these cases. Again, I'm sorry. But there is absolutely nothing we can do. All you can do is to try to keep her comfortable, but recognize that she is gone."

My eyes filled with tears as I cried out, "I simply can't believe it. Can't you examine her? What is the best test for paralysis?" I queried.

The doctor advised that a spinal tap to check for cloudiness of the fluid is usual in such cases, but she reiterated that she was sure the fluid would be clear, and that there would be no physical evidence of anything medically wrong.

"Nevertheless," I replied, my voice shaking with emotion, "please do that test."

Approaching closer to me, she said, "Give me the child." She took the girl into her arms, and said, "All right, I will do the test. But please don't be disappointed if the results are as I told you." I thanked her profusely. She disappeared into the depths of the hospital while Asate's mother and I waited in the vestibule.

About an hour and a half later the doctor appeared in front of us. "As I suspected and told you, we checked the spinal fluid. It was totally clear. There is no medical reason for the child to be paralyzed. You just have to accept the fact that there are things that happen in the bush that we have no way to explain and just have to accept. She'll soon be gone. I'm so sorry. I know that it's hard to accept."

Withering in sadness, I turned to the mother and began trying to explain in Mende. Asate's mother was sad, but she seemed more accepting of the situation than I did. Meanwhile, in fluent Mende, the doctor told her that she would find a place for us to stay and sleep at the hospital that night. Asate's mother and I shared a simple supper of maize porridge meal with the doctor and then were shown to our rooms where we turned in for the night.

Early the next morning, I heard a knock on the door and stumbled sleepily to open it. The doctor was there with a wan and searching look on her face. "Asate died just about an hour ago," she whispered, "and know that she had no pain and passed on peacefully. I noticed that just before she died, she smiled, so she might have been having some happy thoughts before she left us."

I sat down heavily on the bed and put my head between my hands and wept. Tenderly, the doctor sat beside me and put her hand on my shoulder. "The pain will pass, my friend. But it will take time. You must accept what you do not understand."

Later that morning, Asate's mother and I collected her body wrapped in a blanket and we proceeded to the lorry for the return trip home. I'll never forget that her mother uttered not one word all day. Neither did she show sorrow. She was far more accepting of this situation than I was.

The next day, we buried Asate in a simple grave with Pa Bende's immediate neighbors and friends in attendance. I do remember seeing a small tear roll down his face as he shoveled the last of the dirt into the grave.

Even today I still have difficulty accepting how and why Asate died.

# 7.

# Reflections on Community Development

*Stephen M. Bingham*

*The following is an edited version of a longer piece written for family and friends in the United States while I was still a Peace Corps Volunteer (PCV) in Njama, Kowa Chiefdom, Bo District in 1966–67:*

Life here in Njama is more discouraging than anything I've experienced in my life. I have tried on two occasions to have my assignment changed, but those who sit in Freetown have no realistic concept of what we are doing here, what we should be doing, or what is possible for us to do. They live in a world of textbook theories about community development, the same ones in which I so firmly believed 10 short months ago. Everyone you talk to will come up with the same old garbage, "Oh, you don't know what a contribution you are making; you are too close to the situation; you don't see the gradual changes which are taking place."

There have been programs that have succeeded, but not by simply dropping an American down in a random town and saying to him, "You are American, you can succeed. Whatever you do will succeed." What kind of arrogant attitude is this, that we assume the mere presence of an American in the undeveloped world is a positive thing? We live on the economic level of the chief in a society which offers no free rewards, only by hard work, except of course for the corrupt and the inheritors. The people correctly assume that if you're European, you've got it made.

When you've been here six or eight months with no job and no success in getting anyone to do anything by themselves, you begin to try to create a job for yourself. You begin to say, "I can do that for you."

You begin to write the letters to government officials that are supposed to be written by the Native Administrator. You begin to do exactly what community development theory tells you what you must never do: you start doing things *for* the people instead of helping them do things themselves.

Because of community development's slowness and the minimal value of the Volunteer's output, there are more useful places for a Volunteer. Why can't imaginative and constructive programs be worked out to take the fullest advantage of the PCV's capabilities, whether they are in the techniques of growing vegetables, or advice on marketing produce, or engineering, or public administration? This kind of people-to-people approach is meaningful if it is with Africans who at least have pride in themselves and who are successfully educated and holding down a government job. But here in Njama there is often shame because one is black. Try to ask why things are not going so well and people will say, "You see this," tugging at the black skin of their forearms. "We are black people." I once asked a farmer why he sold his rice to the local Lebanese trader rather than to the African trader, and he said "Black man, black heart; white man, white heart. You can't trust the African." Behind that comment lies a long colonial history of self-degradation, as the uneducated African tries to explain how it is that all Europeans he comes in contact with seem to know so much. A really good rice brought in from Njala University College (NUC), a nearby agricultural experiment station, is called *pu be*, meaning European rice. The larger variety of papaya is called English papaya. Only when an African has begun to see improvements that *he has made*, or other more educated Africans have helped him to make, will he gain self-respect, allowing him to accept help from Europeans on an equal footing.

Anything my wife Gretchen Spreckles and I suggest is always approved of as the best idea. Gretchen persuaded people to make beads from local seeds and market them. The thought of wearing local seeds themselves would have seemed too primitive but, after Gretchen walked around for awhile with them on, people wanted their own because they had been accorded approval and recognition by this community's representative of the European world.

We are tampering dangerously with the future of this country's development. As the Freetown staff turns out one more self-concocted scheme after another, from children's agricultural plots to Montessori educational toys, we are entrenching ever more strongly the ingrained feeling that improvement will always come from Europeans.

What is an alternative Peace Corps model? PCVs could train secondary-school-educated Sierra Leoneans to do the kind of work it was envisaged that we PCVs would be doing at the chiefdom level. This would mean working with students at the Kenema Rural Training Institute, teaching them relevant skills and techniques. Although this job is already being done by the staff there, it should be expanded. Similar assistance could be provided at NUC, which is top-heavy with the wrong kind of staff and desperately in need of more practical-minded, younger people who can train agriculturalists on a more hands-on level than that of teacher to student.

The government must be willing to pay a halfway decent salary to those who go to work in small places like Njama. How can I try to force a farm demonstrator to take more interest in his work when he is getting only Le16 per month and has a wife and several children. Gretchen and I are each getting Le 75. Everyone at Njala and Kenema already realizes that the students who don't get jobs with the Produce Marketing Board will find any third-rate clerk's job in any field at all so that they can wear a white shirt and polished shoes. One professor at Njala related that he told his students they were to go on an agricultural field trip the following day and to "dress accordingly." They all showed up in neatly pressed black trousers, black shoes and starched white shirts.

The idea of having PCVs working at such institutions as Kenema Rural Training Institute and NUC should be differentiated from the common concept of the PCV teacher. A staff aide at a place like Njala would spend a great deal of time with his counterpart students outside the classroom. They would work on off-site agricultural projects together and spend long hours after class talking about such currently ignored ideas as the need, value and dignity of working at the local level in agricultural extension. The PCVs would be able to help develop work-study projects, where the Njala students would spend weeks at a time in a small community, helping the people improve their agricultural methods, such as through the introduction of new seed varieties. The PCV could build productive relationships with a number of students, working with each of them at Njala and at the village level.

Of course this is all hypothetical and conceptual, but it provides a framework for a program that not only encourages native Sierra Leoneans to take up the task which their own institutions are training them for, but provides a useful place for the PCV to contribute his talents without replacing Africans or working with uneducated Africans who think all good ideas come from Europeans.

# Epilogue

This was written almost 50 years ago. Curious whether any of the above lessons had been learned over the past few decades, I Googled and found this Peace Corps guide to community development published in 2002: http://multimedia.peacecorps.gov/multimedia/pdf/library/M0069 cedcomplete.pdf . I wonder what has been learned in the intervening decades.

> A business Volunteer was the catalyst who changed the community. He formed a committee of nine villagers and introduced them to the possibilities for community economic development. An impressive entrance to Kubease with a welcome sign was erected. A tourism information center and toilet facilities were built. Houses were re-plastered, and a local artist painted murals depicting African lifestyles on some of the houses. Sidewalks were built, trees planted, and an open pavilion constructed. Village merchants learned what goods and services visitors like and how to provide customer service. A bicycle rental shop opened to serve those who came by bus and wanted to ride rather than walk to the butterfly reserve. Kubease has become a pleasant place where visitors stop and spend some of their money. Citizens enjoy both the new prosperity and improved community environment.

In his example, a PCV savior comes into a village in Ghana and, lo and behold, great things happen. But a critical element is missing from the narrative: whether there was growth among the local Ghanaians' self-respect and self-confidence. Maybe it happened, but we're not told. Until that growth becomes the core outcome of community development projects, we should be suspicious of sending PCVs into rural, uneducated parts of Africa.

# II

# Western Region

## 8.

## A Friend in Need is a Friend Indeed

*Judy and Dwight Sandlin*

When the paramount chief of Koya Chiefdom proved uncooperative, the Peace Corps reassigned us from the small village of Baoma, in the Kenema District, to the Kissy Dockyard area, near Freetown, the capital of Sierra Leone. At the dockyard, Dwight ran a mobile outboard motor repair program in the Fisheries Department, to visit coastal fishing villages and train fishermen in basic maintenance of outboard motors. The Fisheries Department provided a house and a 29-foot diesel fishing and research boat, CARE financed the parts cache on the boat, and the Peace Corps furnished the manpower. Judy conducted an early childhood nutrition program, administered by Oxfam and Catholic Relief Services, in villages around Freetown.

Sometime during our second night in the Kissy Dockyard house, we were burglarized while we slept. Our sense of safety was seriously compromised by the theft and further eroded when Dwight's colleagues at the Fisheries Department told us that the metal thief bars covering all of our windows posed no real barrier to a practiced burglar. Any bars spaced far enough apart to allow a person's head through, would also allow agile, contortionist burglars to slip through the bars into their victims' house. Less agile burglars would reach through the bars with a long, hooked pole and snag items from inside the house. The pole was often covered with rusty razor blades to discourage any homeowner from grabbing it, if he or she happened to awaken.

Our thief had apparently slipped through the thief bars, unlocked our door from the inside, and carted off many of our belongings, most of which were still in moving boxes. Determined to be better prepared, Dwight installed a deadbolt on the front door and began sleeping with a machete by his bed. The new lock required a key to open the door from the inside. He knew it would not totally solve the problem, but it would prevent thieves from carting off our most prized possession, the Peace Corps-issued, kerosene-operated refrigerator.

Just three nights after our first burglary, I was awakened by strange noises. Through the fog of sleep, curiosity slowly seeped into my consciousness. What in the world was going on? Had the natives moved their secret society initiations, with the drums, dancing and screams, into the parlor? In the humid darkness, I listened intently. My eyes focused gradually, and I realized that across the dim room, under the mosquito net, my husband's bed was empty. Something was wrong!

Fear and apprehension hovered at the limits of my consciousness as I ran into the front room. By the eerie light of the moon streaming through uncurtained and unscreened windows, I saw my husband fighting with a dark shadow for the possession of a machete. Since Dwight had installed the deadbolt that required a key to open the door from the inside, thief number two could not escape unless Dwight gave him the key.

Anger battled with fear as the thought flashed through my mind, "How dare some contemptible *tiefman* invade my home again?" I charged into the room and started kicking and clawing. As the thief's hand tightened on my throat, I realized his incredible strength, for Dwight was still pounding away at him. We all three crashed into a wall, and as I picked myself up I knew I would have to find a weapon. With frustration I saw there wasn't one heavy vase or candlestick around our house. I settled for an empty Coca Cola bottle, and ran to the twisting bundle of flesh at the other end of the room. Just as I had seen it enacted in the movies, I brought the bottle down on the thief's head with all of my strength and a sincere desire to kill him. The bottle exploded in a shower of glass, but it had no apparent effect, except that now we were all scuffling around barefooted in broken glass. From sheer desperation I used the only weapon left I could think of; I bit down, hard! Out of the darkness came my husband's cry of pain, and then his unbelievably calm voice, "Judy, you just bit me! Get out of here and go get some help."

Where to go for help was the problem. We had just moved into the house and knew few people on our road. Our nearest neighbor was a trader who lived in a tiny shack in our backyard. I had met him, but I couldn't remember his name, only his tribe. Too desperate to stand on formality, and praying he wouldn't take offense, I screamed out the window, "Hey Fullah man, Help, Help, *tiefman!*"

Suddenly over the rumpus, I heard a pounding on the steel door in back. It took me what seemed like endless minutes to undo the locks. With the clank of the last bolt, the door flew open. Silhouetted against the black night was a man almost as black. The moonlight flashed from a huge saber in his hand. Without a word he jumped into the battle, and I ran out the door to summon the family across the road.

As I pounded at the door, men, women, and children began pouring out of the house and stood jabbering on the porch. I instinctively repeated the three words that would overcome the language barrier between their African-Lebanese and my English, "*Tiefman*, Help, *Tiefman.*" An older man, obviously the patriarch of the clan, came onto the porch and with great interest began to discuss the situation, "Oh, you say there is a thief man in your house. Is he there now?" In my muddled brain the significance of the conversation finally registered. The man and most of his family understood me perfectly. They had no intention of coming to our aid. With disgust, I left the porch and ran back home. I had no clear plan, but I was too worried to stay away longer.

I need not have worried. Lying in the mud of our backyard was my gentle, soft-spoken husband, with a firm choke hold on the thief's throat. The Fullah trader stood nearby, and periodically gave the thief a kick in the ribs. To our surprise, police arrived shortly on the scene. Since the Afro-Lebanese family had the only telephone in the neighborhood, we assumed that they had notified the authorities.

After the police took the thief away in handcuffs, Dwight filled me in on the excitement I had missed. It seems the Fullah, Mohammedu, had charged in like a Sherman tank. The battle had progressed from the front room, through the kitchen, and into the yard. The back door, made of steel, was knocked from its hinges in the process.

Somewhat in shock, we stumbled back inside the house. By the glare of the one fluorescent light, we could see large patches of blood that smeared the white walls and marked the trail of the fight. Only then did I realize that Dwight was bleeding. Since it was 3:00 a.m., we knew we would have to wait four or five hours to find transportation to medical help. Using my training as an Army medic and with the Peace Corps first aid kit, we were able to stop the bleeding.

With the arrival of daylight, we traveled by *poda-poda* to the Peace Corps office in the Congo Cross area of Freetown. There, "Doctor Steve" treated Dwight's wounds. Anticipating future legal proceedings, the doctor narrated a list of Dwight's injuries into his tape recorder: "machete cuts along left forearm and base of fingers, deep stab wound in left thigh, severe abrasions on soles of both feet, and … human bite marks on back?" Chagrined, I had to confess that I, not the thief, had made the teeth marks. Everybody in the Peace Corps office, including Harry Kightlinger, the assistant director, gathered to examine Dwight's wounds and listen to our story. Harry said he would represent us in court, if we were summoned. News traveled upcountry by the jungle grapevine, which proved surprisingly efficient in this case. Within days, volunteers in the remotest hinterlands knew about our adventure.

For security reasons, Dr. Steve insisted that we check in to the Peace Corps hostel, in downtown Freetown, for a few days. Dwight, with both feet bandaged to prevent infection (always a worry in the tropics), was instructed to rest and stay off his feet. At the end of a long day, Dwight volunteered to sleep in the top bunk. I had just turned off the light and settled into the lower bunk when he cried out "something is crawling on my feet!" Switching the light back on, I saw that his bandaged feet were now black with a moving mass: bedbugs! Drawn by the scent of blood, the bedbugs covered the soles of Dwight's feet. Fortunately, thick bandages protected the wounds. We discovered bugs nesting in the seams of our mosquito nets. Choosing to risk a malarial mosquito bite rather than another bedbug attack, we scraped the bugs off his feet and disposed of them, along with the infested mosquito nets. We returned to bed for a few hours

Within a few days the Peace Corps reinstated their policy of paying for night watchmen in urban areas. We hired a local native watchman and returned to our Kissy Dockyard home. Several weeks later we were notified to appear in court. We were ushered into the courtroom, to stand before a female native magistrate, resplendent in her black robes and curly, white judicial wig, patterned after the British legal system. Without explanation, the bailiff escorted me out of the courtroom while Dwight told the story of his encounter with the thief. When Dwight reached the part where the thief threatened to kill him, the proceedings came to an abrupt halt. The magistrate sentenced the man to two years in prison. It seems that the court was well acquainted with the thief and his previous criminal record.

In 1967, Sierra Leone experienced military coups and much political unrest. Our trader friend, Mohammedu, was threatened by rioting locals who wanted to batter their way into his shop and steal all the merchandise. They spent one night pounding on his shop's corrugated metal ("pan") walls with clubs and stones, terrifying him as he tried to sleep on the small cot in the back of his shop. Mohammedu wanted to get out of the area until the "trouble" subsided, and asked if we would store the contents of his shop in our house. We were grateful for the chance, in a small way, to return his friendship. We helped him move a few burlap bags of tinned food, crackers, cigarettes, Vimto and other soft drinks into our house, and placed them out of sight from any window.

As the political problems worsened, the military overthrew the civilian government. The Peace Corps Sierra Leone Director, George Taylor, gathered all of the Freetown-area volunteers to his house up in the diplomatic region to escape the rioting. After a second military coup, the situation improved enough that we were able to return to our home in the dockyard. The house was intact, and Mohammedu's goods were still there. We were delighted to find that he too had survived. We helped him restock and reopen his shop.

Though we frequently found our night watchman asleep on the job, we had no further burglary incidents. The smaller wire mesh that the Fisheries Department welded over our thief bars probably helped, too. We completed our two-year tour and returned to the United States.

We never heard of our friend Mohammedu again, but we have thought about him often. The incident in which he played such an important role is still vivid in our memories. Our view of the current conflicts with Muslims around the world is tempered by our experience of this man who transcended differences in language, race, religion, and culture to come to the aid of strangers. Our being friends in need, he was clearly a friend, indeed.

In 1986, during a twenty-fifth anniversary celebration of the Peace Corps that we helped organize in Anchorage, Alaska, we met a young man who had just returned from his Peace Corps assignment. He had served in the Sierra Leone Fisheries Department, had used the same 29-foot diesel fishing boat that Dwight had used, and he had visited some of the same fishing villages that Dwight had served.

From our Peace Corps service, we retain an avid interest in world events. The entire experience provided us with a new appreciation for the complexities of life: the good and bad, the differences and similarities between people, politics, and events. Our lives have been deeply influenced by our time in the Peace Corps. We continue to volunteer on a variety of community projects, remembering that locally as well as globally, it is always better to be part of the solution than part of the problem.

# III

# Eastern Region

# 9.

## Two Episodes and a Poem

*Doc Long*

The red, white, and blue poster proclaimed, "Now that you have a degree, why not get an education." It was a bold, intrusive challenge and an invitation to adventure, self–revelation, and the reshaping of one's worldview. It was the mid-1960s, and the turbulent swift winds of idealism were sweeping the nation. I was 23 years old and game for a challenge.

Before I knew it, I was a Peace Corps volunteer in the rainforest and swamps of Sierra Leone, working with local farmers. Did I do any good for the people by merely helping to clear swampland and introducing a few new ideas about farming? Did I make a difference in anyone's life? I don't know, but I do know that I did get an education and a broader understanding of how the world works and how the politics of my life have been shaped. The words on the poster were prophetic.

Among the many volumes of experiences that jarred my imagination during my tour, I want to share two stellar moments.

## Goats and freight trains

I was walking back from the marketplace in Kenema, the capital of the Kenema District, on my way to the Peace Corps rest house where I spent the night once a month after buying provisions to take back to my compound, some 25 bush-miles south. Suddenly I heard an outcry, something like one might hear at a sporting event, say, a soccer or cricket match, or when a crowd had chased down and caught a thief and flogged him until the police came to his rescue. The uproar sounded something like that, but this time it wouldn't be for any of those reasons. Ahead I saw people rushing from different directions toward the railroad tracks in back of the local post office. I moved toward the commotion, dodging and weaving my way between people and lorries packed with travelers and animals clogging the narrow streets. I walked and half jogged around to the north side of the post office, which faced the train tracks. A throng of people, mostly women, were running down into a small gully, screaming and shouting. They were carrying large metal pans or basins in their hands or on their heads, scrambling in excitement along the railroad tracks. Some were crawling on their hands and knees, slipping and stumbling along the sloping banks along the tracks. Some had lost their shoes or sandals and ran in bare feet. They were mumbling in excitement, with an entranced urgency. Women from the nearby marketplace, dressed in bright-colored tie-dyed *gaylays* and deftly tied head wraps, swarmed the tracks with emptied tin pans, scooping up chunks of slaughtered goat meat, blood splashing on their dresses, running down their arms, dripping onto their sandals, and mixing with the dust on their feet. They snatched up iridescent strands of meat, pearl-colored gristle of bones, blue-sinewed twitching lumps of blood, and bulging eyes from the steel railroad tracks and then slung rags of meat into tin tubs with their bare, blood-stained hands. They were heaving long strings of pink intestines, balloon-shaped clots of blood, and massive rags of flesh into tin pans that had only minutes ago had held oranges, mounds of rice, or plantain. Disemboweled, beheaded goats lay split open, body parts still panting in trauma, a slaughterhouse at mid-day. One woman ran along the tracks with a goat's head in a pan she carried atop her head, an eye and tongue bulging out at the confusion.

Goat meat was strewn along the railroad tracks for at least a hundred yards, where 20, maybe 30 goats had been slaughtered by the 2:15 freight train passing through the heart of the city. Its arrival had caught a local farmer's herd of goats crossing the tracks. Buzzards circled. Scrawny lean dogs lapped skin from the metal spikes of the tracks. Insects gathered and alighted on blood-soaked gravel, staking their share of the bounty. The farmer, in a maniacal fury, had rounded up the few remaining goats that had escaped the massacre and stood dejected on a nearby hillside. The train, having never stopped or slowed, eased silently down the tracks and out of sight.

In a few moments the commotion would settle, and the afternoon would float back into its slow bustling energy. The sun glared and bounced off of the tin roof tops of buildings, gleaming immovable and intense, as if nothing had happened. Green flies swarmed and darted through the air. I continued my walk back to the rest house.

## At the bottom of the well

Before I could think it, speculate, or begin to suggest it to myself, Hugh McAllorum had stripped down to his underwear and was standing at approximately 8 degrees north of the Equator, in the middle of a rainforest, on a Wednesday afternoon, surrounded by a small group of Mende tribesmen. Hugh, Lucky Strike-smoking, guitar-playing, knee pants-wearing, shit-talking, and long beer drinking Hugh McAllorum, stood there, in his Fruit of the Looms, as white as a spectre from Ireland in the middle of the coffee groves and coca plantations in Black Africa. He stood surrounded by a host of black men, who for the moment were consumed and smothered in audacious silence and surprise, everyone looking first at a near-naked Hugh, then down at the black hole in the earth, then back again at Hugh .

Here's how it all came to this classic moment in the middle of our tour as Peace Corps volunteers. Earlier that morning Hugh had stopped by my compound and picked me up to attend a ceremony for the completion of a well and the final installation of the pump that he and local villagers had dug and constructed over the past year. He would connect the pump handle that had arrived at long last and thus complete the project. Arriving at the well site, where a small crowd had already gathered, he got out of the truck. Hugh reached into the bed of the truck and got the pump handle, which was still packed in the box it had been carted in, marked U.S.A.I.D. Somehow, between unpacking the box and attaching the handle to the pump, it slipped from Hugh's hand and fell into the well. That's right: it fell to the bottom of the well.

A rope, a vine, a line, or a cord from heaven appeared. I don't recall exactly where it came from, but before I knew it, Hugh was being lowered down into the well in nothing but his underwear. I cringed as his head disappeared into the hole in the Earth. There was my fellow PCV at the bottom of a well, thousands of miles from home. If something went wrong, I would hold myself partly responsible, but there had been no other alternative, certainly not one that came to mind before he was eased down into the abyss. "You OK?" I bleated, almost without realizing it. "Yeah!" came back a muted reply, an echo amidst splashing water and darkness. Then there was more splashing, followed by silence. I could hear him gasping for breath, silence, splashing, and more breathing. "Pull me up, pull me up," his voice came up through the hole in the ground. Immediately the rope tightened and the villagers began to haul Hugh up out of the well. "Couldn't find the damn thing." He emerged dripping with water, reaching for his pants, shirt, and a cigarette all at the same time.

I don't know what made me do it, and I don't know if I would do it again, but I stripped down and in an instant was lowered into the well, feet and knees scrapping against the cemented sides, and then eventually I touched down in the cool darkness. I could feel the soft freshness of the water rushing up from the underground spring, a current of mystery. I looked up and could make out blurred faces staring down at me, imposed against a blue circle of sky and light. I let go of the rope, took a deep breath, and did a surface dive down into the darkness. Immediately the force of water pushing upward from the underground cavity pushed me back to the surface. I hadn't even touched the bottom and had no idea of how deep the bottom might have been. Like waves in the ocean, there was a turbulence beneath the surface. Again I dove under, blind and pushing against the current, kicking and waving my arms, pumping and kicking, one time, two times, three, still no bottom. I reversed my body and headed back up to the surface, being hurled by the upward goad of the current. I broke through to the surface and heard the commotion of voices coming from the circle of faces above me. Hugh broke in, "Doing all right?"

"Yeah, let me give it one more try" I yelled in echo, forcing words past water in my nose and mouth. Deep breath in, surface dive, pump the arms, kick the feet, cheeks bulged with air, one, two, three, four times, I fanned the water and kicked down pulling against the current, down until finally my hand struck the sandy bottom of the well. I blindly patted the sand and gravel, feeling around from side to side still kicking my feet in order to stay submerged and anchored. Then suddenly my hand struck the numb dead steel of the pump handle. I grabbed it and fought my way back up toward the surface of light. "Got it!" I caught my breath and yelled at the circle of faces at the top of the darkness, and a commotion of celebration lit the air.

Later, back at the compound, Hugh and I sat listening to Bob Dylan on a battery-operated record player singing something about *"the pump don't work 'cause the vandals took the handle."* We poured

another cup of palm wine from a gourd and talked about how in a few
months we would be stateside, back in the U.S. of A.

## Ghana '67

I bit the apple
but I didn't inhale
didn't drink the cool aide
but said the prayer
I told but didn't tell
didn't take the red pill
didn't take the blue one
saw mercy at the gate of latitudes and vectors
how many prayers in a grain of sand
how many slave ships in a sunset?
Accra, and Black Star Square
the tomb of Dubois,
and I told you so
Nkrumah had fled to Guinea
cancer nagging at his blood.
Stokely, articulating Kwame Toure
Barack Obama was just six years old.
King's death, a year away, Malcolm already gone
wasted on the Audubon dance floor
Baldwin in the silence
at the center of darkness.
Ali and Frazier had not yet fought
Assassinations and universes wobbling in orbit
the beginning of where I would never return from.
You too angry, so hurt, so this, you that,
history, mystery, so fire, so god young man.
A one-eyed guard dog at the airport gate
aims his rifle at my head
and pushes me into real time.
This is not the game I played as a child
if upcountry, I am Hausa from Nigeria
and a slaughtered casualty of war.
In the village I explain my tribe and the slave trade
they weep and offer shelter
where is your mother, your father

are there others like you in America
let them come here and bring their sorrow
ancestors in lockstep stomp dust from the earth.
Blend with the night sky,
become the skin of water
kente cloth and palm butter
taste blood on cassava, blood on rice
remain silent like troubled mountains.
Live long enough and witness your own rebirth
where even flaws diamond in compassionate light
time, and the cola nuts are bitter sweet.

## Lessons and reasons

Engaging *culture shock;* living in another country and making adjustments to its culture and way of life. Adjusting to a new concept of time, stepping out of the New York minute into the upcountry minute. Never mind exactness, now one settled for approximations, and being comfortable with the general as opposed to the specific. Time was measured by morning, afternoon, or evening, not with the exactness of 9:15, 1:30, or 6:45. How might the goat farmer have fared better if he had known the train schedule, or if the train itself had run according to an exact schedule? Commerce and politics hadn't demanded such punctuality. If we hadn't retrieved the pump handle we would have had to wait another six months or more for a new one to arrive.

Leopold Senghor and Aime Cesaire coined the term *negritude,* and the historian Lerone Bennett, Jr., had underscored it as *a certain dark joy.* An unspoken kinship, a connectedness found throughout the African Diaspora that was to be found in the literature, the music, the tonal quality of languages, certain patterns of logic, in the foods, and the shared history of oppression and separation, and the suppressed Africanisms found wherever the dispersal of African peoples had taken root.

At the same time, it had been W.E.B. Dubois who had recognized and spoken of the duality of consciousness existing among blacks who were at once African and American. We were outsiders, as it were, yet insiders at the same time. However, there would be no returning to the culture and ways of the past. I had been hundreds of years removed, yet ironically, back in the United States the cry for cultural nationalism, Black Power, and the surge of black consciousness were blooming and gaining momentum. But here on The Continent I had come to the awareness that I was more American than I had realized.

# 10.
## Vultures on the Roof

*Milton Lane*

W e arrived at Sierra Leone's Lungi Airport in January 1966 in the midst of West Africa's dry season. To reach Freetown from Lungi, we took a ferry and a lorry. It was during this trip that my anxious enthusiasm was suddenly dampened by the awful stench we encountered upon entering the city. I remember telling myself, "Let's go home. I'm not going to make it." I would later learn that the offensive odor was caused by a poor sewage system, worsened by a lack of rain and swamp-like conditions.

After a few days of orientation at Fourah Bay College, we sought out our designated assignments. As we left Freetown for the hinterland, the stench seemed to disappear. Months later, upon my return for "R&R," I would find the city to be a delightful place in spite of the stench which, by then, had all but disappeared, due to the rains. Had I listened to myself, I would have missed out on a key life-changing experience.

Because my family never owned an automobile, there was no reason for me to learn to drive. My first real experience with a motor vehicle came at age 22 in the backcountry of Sierra Leone, West Africa. The Peace Corps assigned me to the remote town of Kailahun, near the Liberian border. Before he departed, my predecessor essentially taught me everything there was to know about an old gray Land Rover: how to change the oil, how to change the spark plugs, how to dismantle and disassemble the engine, and foremost, how to drive it. The latter I learned the hard way, and I strongly recommend that all prospective drivers learn first on a manual transmission.

For a novice such as myself, it was quite a chore to manually shift gears in concert with road conditions, as well as the speed of oncoming vehicles. Most of the country's roads, other than those approaching major towns such as Freetown, Bo, Kenema, Makeni, and Koidu Town, were unpaved and barely wide enough for two vehicles to pass one another. During the rainy season, they were often impassable for days on end as lorries of various sizes attempted to free themselves from the thick laterite mud. Heavy dry-season traffic left them dusty and heavily scarred with corrugation. Even the more seasoned drivers had been known to struggle with the navigation of said roads. Insert a 22-year-old first-time driver into the above scenario, and an accident was soon to occur.

On my way to Pendembu on the Kailahun-to-Pendembu road, I encountered a bald-tired mammy wagon overloaded with passengers and livestock headed in the opposite direction. Emerging from a blind turn, we were both probably traveling too fast. As we both veered to the left to avoid colliding, we found ourselves capsized on opposite sides of the road. Fortunately, there were no serious injuries and I would survive many more such incidents, often "shaken but not stirred." This was the origin of my becoming the butt of a number of "OO7" references initiated by the Hugh McAllorums and the Doc Longs of the world.

## Nancy's Place

I drove to Makeni to pick up a pup named Brutus, promised to me by Nancy Lederer. To my surprise, she lived next to the town marketplace. Exhausted after the long drive from Kailahun, I slept deeply into the early dawn, until I was suddenly awakened by loud thumping noises on the roof. Nancy later informed me that the thumping sounds were made by vultures attracted by the freshly slaughtered meat in the marketplace. Fancy my being united with Brutus in a "vulture's nest!"

# 11.

## A Kono Experience

*Rev. John H. Cole*

*Dedicated to Ann Himelick Cole, 1941–1982, who was also there.*

Ann and I were tired when we finally reached Freetown on January 9, 1966. It had been a long flight from New York to Dakar and then on to Conakry, where we boarded Air Guinea for the final leg to Sierra Leone. Descending through the yellow-tan dust of the Harmattan wind, we were thankful that the Czechoslovak instructors, whom we could see through the open cockpit door pointing to dials, were successful in their training. It was bumpy, but we landed safely. In the Freetown guest house we managed to get some much-needed sleep in spite of the pye dogs howling all night long. Kono, in the Eastern Province, was still many days away, and Kayima, headquarters of Sando Chiefdom, where we were assigned, was almost at the end of the road.

The next step was training, up on the heights overlooking the city. It was cooler up there, a relief from the enormous heat of Freetown, which is why the white and the rich preferred to live there. The city below was a jumble of shacks with tin roofs, old colonial buildings, lorries, vendors, paved streets with open sewers, very friendly people, and beggars, one with no legs on a rolling cart. We saw more "in your face" poverty during those first days in the city than we had seen even in the two years we had spent working in central Harlem. In Freetown we met a number of important people including the Peace Corps director, the medical people, and Bob Golding, the CARE–Peace Corps program director.

We were a community development project that had linkage with CARE, but most of our training, at Hampton Institute and in St. Croix,

77

was in agriculture. There was some training in building; we learned to work with cement and bricks in St. Croix and were instructed in using a machine to make bricks out of mud. However, the balance of what training we received was in basic agriculture. At Hampton, for example, I remember learning about fruit trees from a wonderful old African-American man who was about all that was left of their agricultural college days. His special love was peaches. In St. Croix a somewhat sadistic U.S. Agriculture Department representative had us pick hot peppers without gloves and showed us some huge avocado trees. In general, the training we received did little to help once I was at my assignment. Watching pigs being slaughtered at the Smithfield Ham factory near Hampton may have prepared me for seeing animals killed for food in Kono, but I am not sure. The main support I remember from CARE was tool kits of shovels and wrenches, which had some limited usefulness when we finally received them.

Finally on the road out of Freetown, going northeast first to Kenema and then on to diamond country and our new home in Sando, the reality of upcountry transportation kicked in when we discovered the road was paved for only a few miles outside the capital. A two-lane dirt road was the main link from there to the entire eastern part of the country. It's a good thing that the main products of the eastern mining operations, diamonds, were small enough to be easily flown out. Lorries of all types jammed the roads: the Bedfords with families on benches carrying all their goods, including animals; the little blue Renault buses, Land Rovers, tanker trucks, and the "big men" with their Mercedes. If someone broke down or went off the road, the whole line of traffic came to a halt while the situation was sorted out. Everyone complained and had an opinion, but everyone helped. During the rainy season, problems multiplied, and getting stuck in the mud was a frequent issue; the season of rain was a good time to stay close to home. Good weather or bad, your ride stopped periodically so that the devout Muslims could get out and place their prayer rugs beside the road for their devotions. I learned that during Ramadan there was an additional danger as Muslims were fasting, some not even swallowing their own saliva. Spitting out of an open vehicle–most had no window glass–at speed could cause problems. From time to time protests were shouted, "Hey, Bo, control your spit do ya!"

We stayed a few days in the PC rest house in Kenema, where we learned the wonders of groundnut stew, made with palm oil, chicken, peanuts, and pepper. We also met the last British provincial secretary, a Mr. Fenal, who did not seem to fit the image of an ugly colonial type but was soon leaving his post as the position was becoming "more political." Another British man, the provincial agriculture officer, spent time bringing us up to speed on coffee, cacao, and rice. He was disappointed that we did not have better training in tropical agriculture, believing that was the most important need in the country at the time.

## Diamond Cowboys

The long and dusty road finally got us to Koidu town, where we began to see what impact diamonds really had on the country. While in Kenema, we had visited the official diamond buying office, approved by the national government and run by the Sierra Leone Selection Trust (SLST), a subsidiary of DeBeers, the South African diamond monopoly. A pile of what appeared to be small glass chips, some clear but most somewhat yellow, were the innocent-looking producers of both wealth and despair. Young men from all over Sierra Leone flooded the area in the hope of becoming rich finding these things. In Koidu town, successful finders of a stone or two would buy a vehicle and become urban cowboys overnight. The streets where full of these guys, ready to take you and all you could haul, anywhere, at any time. Each "taxi" or truck was colorfully decorated and had really great West African music blaring. The energy of the place was amazing, and there seemed to be plenty of folks with money to spend at the numerous markets and at the big downtown movie theater, where knock-off James Bond and American cowboy movies were very popular.

Entry into the Kono District was restricted, with official checkpoints to look at papers, but many people walked in on the unpatrolled bush paths anyway. I learned the term "Kono stoop," which described the way folks would walk through the unpaved streets here, occasionally finding a stone that had dropped from the big SLST truck that brought gravel into the large processing plant in the town. Tons of gravel, dug out of well-guarded bends in the major rivers in Kono, were carefully screened in order to find the few pieces of precious rock washed downstream over centuries. Some local Kono folks were employed by SLST in this enterprise, but many more, legal and illegal, were from out of the district and the country, in spite of the restrictions.

A contingent of South Africans were in charge and lived in a very Western-style compound north of the town in a place called Koidu and another called Yengama. In Yengama, there was a company store with imported products for those who could pay the price and a secondary school where a number of Peace Corps teachers were assigned. All diamonds were either captured by the large-scale industrial process described above or, if found by individuals, were to be sold only to the company. However, there were better ways to unload your diamonds. We later met Jamil, "Beautiful" in Arabic, an Afro-Lebanese who was the main illicit diamond buyer in the Kono District. A very slick-looking and charming guy, he had the attitude and quiet power of a New York mob boss. We met him through the branch manager of the short-lived Inter Bank, a Lebanese institution with a lot of influence in West Africa at the time. He offered better prices than the SLST folks and smuggled the diamonds out of country to Monrovia, Liberia.

## The end of the road at last

Finally, after almost a month in country, we went the last 40 miles to Kayima, the chiefdom headquarters of Sando. There were more dirt roads closed in by the bush, small villages, and a major river to cross. The ferry, hand-pulled by ropes, was owned by SLST and was open to the public when the company was not using it. Vendors selling peeled oranges and cooked food were on both sides to provide for those waiting in line. Here, as in most other places in the country, travel was an exercise in patience. African time was slower than our usual pace, and you arrived at your destination whenever you could.

In Sando chiefdom, older folks and those on the major road had seen white folks before, but young people had not. Women loved to thrust kids into our arms just to see their reaction. Our town was beautiful. As we came down the hill where the rest house was located, under huge cotton and mango trees, the village was neatly laid out along the road with a river on the near side. Most of the compounds and the court *barre* were made from clay and mud, sometimes with a coating of cement, and roofed with corrugated metal, "pan." We stayed first in the rest house until they could finish whitewashing our house, which was on the far side of town, separated from the more densely packed houses by a small brook. With open land around it, it had about six rooms, including a store that could be opened up on the porch in the front. With much more room than we needed, the house belonged to J.O. Sorie, the chief's brother and one of the richest men in the country. He had a compound on the other side of the road beyond ours and occasionally visited his wives there, coming into town with his entourage of bodyguards and assistants in his black Mercedes. He mainly stayed in Freetown, and I met him only twice during my two years in Kayima.

Eventually moving into our own house and finally locating the furniture provided, we set up our bed with the required nets, and our kerosene stove, refrigerator, and lanterns. With all our books and good-ies, we were clearly among the few educated elite in the area. We met Sergeant Major Blake, a Krio man, in charge of the national police compound just beyond our house; the teachers in the Evangelical United Brethren (EUB) elementary school we passed on the way into town; and the chiefdom headquarters clerk, Mr. Konomani. This tall young man, about my age, was the link between the national govern-ment and the administration of the paramount chief who, with his advi-sors and sub-chiefs, was clearly in charge of everything in Sando. Konomani spoke English well and had about a junior high school edu-cation and a great sense of humor. He wanted to learn as much as pos-sible from me and welcomed Ann and me into his home. Once, eating the main noonday meal with him, which consisted of some kind of bush meat with cassava leaves pounded with pepper and red palm oil, he, with a twinkle in his eye, opened his fridge to show us a plate of mon-key arms, explaining that we had eaten the rest.

## Chief Fasiloco-Sonsiamo, MBE, OBE

We had been told that the paramount chief was a jolly old man who spoke no English. He and his elders greeted us with great fanfare, welcoming us with the gift of a live sheep, which I had trouble know-ing what to do with. This "dash" (something between a gift and a bribe, given with some expectation of return) was intended to be eaten, and I am sure I was expected to give a big party for everyone. But it took me so long to figure out what to do with the sheep, which was tethered for a few weeks outside my house, that it was acquired by someone else, perhaps the original owner, and, I am sure, put to good use. After a while, I discovered that the chief understood and could speak just as much English as he wished, although perhaps not per-fectly. He also spoke Fulani, Mende, Temne, Koranko, Limba, and Kissi, as well as his native language, Kono. He claimed to remember a few words of French and German he had picked up over the years and had participated in a few years of mission school early in the 20th cen-tury. He was at the time over 80, a wise old fox with a twinkle in his eye. He was deeply concerned about the civil war in Nigeria, fearing that the kind of reaction to traditional authority he saw there could spread in West Africa and threaten the very institutions he represented. Despite the presence of Konomani and the Sergeant Major, he was the recognized authority here. He was nominally a Muslim, and with about 80 wives, he was connected by marriage to nearly all the important families in his chiefdom.

His power came in part from the periodic assignment of farm plots throughout the area. Under the slash-and-burn system of agriculture, families had to move their cultivated land at least every two to three years so that the bush and trees that were cut down and burned at the end of the dry season could be re-established. This regrowth was at least a 10-to-15-year process, so land use was always shifting. The chief knew where all of the family groups traditionally farmed and, with his advisors, assigned new plots when the old ones had to be left fallow. He received a portion of the rice production from these farms and could make life hard for a family or group that he was vexed with. His other power, which could conflict with the national government, was to settle disputes. He did this regularly in the court *barre* in Kayima. National judges were few in number and often located only in the district headquarters, and it took time and money (a "dash" was expected) to expect settlement from them, so the chiefdom court was more popular.

## Rice and wealth

At the time we were there, the local economy was based on agriculture. If you did not grow food, you did not eat. In Sando, folks usually had enough rice, with some left for sale and for use as seed rice. If for some reason the rains were not so good or something went wrong, things could get bad quickly, but during our time we did not see this. Many varieties of dried fish, *bonga*, were trucked up from the coast, which was one source of protein in addition to bush meat. "Malinki men" from the Kabala area, in Koinadugu District, drove small herds of cattle down from the north. They were referred to as "Kabala traffic cops" when they blocked the main roads on their way to Koidu Town, the capital of Kono District. A few ended up slaughtered in our town on the way and were hung up for sale. The meat required a lot of cooking; those northern cows were tough!

Bush meat, like the above-mentioned monkey, was available and much desired in the cooking pot, but the base of every meal was rice. The large dish in the middle of the table was mounded with freshly pounded and cooked upland rice and covered with red (palm oil and pepper) and green (cassava leaves or other greens), pounded with salt and some kind of fish or meat. At the table men sat with men and women with women, unless Ann was with me. I learned to love the flavors and to this day, I miss the experience. The rice was almost always grown on the sides of the hills that covered most of our area; there was very little flat area available.

Trees were cut down on a new plot every two years or so and burned at the end of the dry season. The air was saturated with ash from the burning. The work required to do this was enormous, and the bigger the trees cut down, the better the thin tropical soil was considered to be for rice growing. Seed rice was then broadcast over the area, and with the advent of the rains the rice grew and was harvested near the end of the rainy season. Whole families went out to their farms to work on these plots, and depending on the time of year, most were there throughout the day. Boys sometimes stayed full time in small thatch huts to chase away birds and protect the growing rice from rodents. The *kwedine*, "rice child," a woodchuck-like beast, not only likes new rice shoots but is a favorite bush meat ingredient in everyone's cooking pot.

Part of what I ended up doing during my two years in Sando Chiefdom was encouraging a different type of rice cultivation. Working with a Dutchman from the Food and Agriculture Organisation, we attempted to have folks build bunds around the swamps and use high-yielding swamp rice seed. This was somewhat successful, and if it had been continued it could have created a more stable and less ecologically damaging method of growing rice. One of my treks took me to the far north of the chiefdom, where after passing a conical mound where active sacrifice took place, we emerged onto the savanna, which stretches from the border of Kono to the deserts of Timbuktu. I wonder how far this border has moved south over the years into the West African forest as the slash-and-burn system continues to create more arid conditions.

## Endings

After about nine months of trying to be an informal home economics teacher, Ann was officially allowed by the Peace Corps and the government to teach in the elementary school in town. Teaching was a far more satisfying experience, and she felt she really made a difference. At the end of my two years, I was a lot less clear about the impact I made. I hope there was some change in the way folks thought about growing rice, but I am not sure. However, the two years were a great experience for both of us. The people of Sando were wonderful and always remain fondly in my memory.

Sadly, we could see during our time there that major change was coming. The paramount chief's fear about his authority being eroded was all too justified. The days were numbered for the institutions that he represented. Our last few weeks in the country saw the end of Albert Margai's term as prime minister, an office he had held since Sierra Leone's independence, and the rejection of the elections that voted in a new party. The Sierra Leone Peoples Party was supplanted by Siaka Stevens and the All People's Congress. Then a series of military coups started just as we left. Although these changes were at first relatively bloodless, in the years since then, tragic events have piled up, leaving Kono a devastated remnant of the district I experienced when I was there. I expect the roots of the "Blood Diamond" tragedy were there then: lack of good education, poverty just under the surface, and the "cowboy" mentality that encouraged grabbing as much as possible in an exploitive and corrupt system.

I don't know if I will ever dare to return to Kono. The population is only one-third of what it was when Ann and I were there. I can't even find some towns in Sando on Google Earth any more. I guess at some level I need to look at the roots and seeds of what occurred there, and I may do so one day.

# 12

# What Did Our Peace Corps Service Mean?

*Roger B. Hirschland*

With my furry gray pet monkey named Fuzz perched on my forearm, I watched a bulldozer operator drag one vehicle after another up a steep stretch of hill. The road consisted of sticky red mud some 24 inches deep. This was Sierra Leone's main cross-country highway back in 1966, and the West African rains had turned it into an impassible morass. As a Peace Corps volunteer riding a local conveyance back to my village up-country, monkey in tow, I was one of hundreds of travelers stuck at the mercy of the bulldozer driver. When frustrated drivers who had waited as long as four hours yelled tribal-based insults at the operator, he would shut down his machine until the proper amends were made, and the messy operation would resume.

Fuzz and I eventually made it back to my village—a village far from everywhere. I had studied indigenous cultures while majoring in anthropology, and in seeking to live with an indigenous group, had asked the Peace Corps to give me as remote an assignment as possible. The Peace Corps was more obliging than I could have hoped, and I was placed for two years in a village of mud huts that I reached by crossing the entire country of Sierra Leone, then proceeding along a 37-mile-long tortuous double-track dirt road. It wound and dived through rain forest and 12-foot-high grasses in the hilly savanna of northeastern Sierra Leone, ending—at last—in the small town of Saiama, population 300.

The grassy hills and serenity of this remote spot were addictive. The people were kind and open to working together, even though when I first arrived, I didn't even know how to say hello in the local language, Kono. In a population where half the children were dying of tetanus, malnutrition, dehydration, and parasites before the age of five—and adults were succumbing to hernias and rabies—the villagers were eager to learn ways to improve their health. They also hoped their Peace Corps volunteer could help them increase their yield of rice and build a bridge that would extend their road across the local river so trucks, rather than men, could tote the 100-pound sacks of coffee beans and rice to market from outlying communities even smaller than Saiama.

The experience of being deposited in the middle of an unfamiliar culture in an unfamiliar climate in an unfamiliar land has affected my knowledge, my values, my capacity for patience, and my outlook ever since. For the 45 years since my return, I have taught junior high school, edited children's magazines at National Geographic, given countless slide shows to students, and helped produce geography and cross-cultural materials at Peace Corps headquarters for U.S. school-children, in an effort to convey to others the remarkable things I learned in my little tropical village.

Although love and hunger and envy and laughter are things that my Sierra Leonean friends and I experienced in common, our sense of time, of schedules, of urgency, for example, could not have been more different. Arriving for a meeting 24 hours late is not a big deal in Sierra Leone; in Washington, D.C., where I live now, it raises eyebrows. This kind of disparity between the two cultures is real and profound, and understanding that people think, operate, and function differently from me was crucial in helping me understand others around me when I came home. Peace Corps volunteers learn quickly about the cultures that they join.

I guess that's what caused me to gravitate toward producing edu-cational materials for U.S. students, focused on cross-cultural issues. It is essential for students to understand the profound differences among cultures from other parts of the world. In U.S. classrooms that more and more represent the different cultures of the globe, and in a world in which cross-cultural understanding will likely determine the success or failure of our international relations, what more important issue is there than training our students to understand people who are different from us?

As a returned Peace Corps volunteer, I spent more than 20 years at the National Geographic Society, writing and editing in the hope of instilling in young readers an understanding of cultures enormously different from my own. My professional path finally led me back to the Peace Corps, where as editor in the Domestic Programs division, I worked with a cadre of enthusiastic colleagues whose sole professional purpose was to help educate U.S. students about far pockets of the world. How did we do it?

Our effort was the Coverdell World Wise Schools program. Conceived by then-Peace Corps Director Paul D. Coverdell in 1989, the program was initially designed to link Peace Corps volunteers in the field with U.S. classrooms as a way of helping volunteers in culturally different places share their experiences with U.S. schoolchildren while still "on the ground" at their assigned sites.

The program was an instant hit. Today, that early Correspondence Match program is still thriving, with some 4,000 Volunteers communicating with an estimated 200,000 students in the United States at any one time. But World Wise Schools widened its efforts by producing written and oral materials that describe the cross-cultural issues Peace Corps volunteers face in the field on a daily basis and also address issues crucial in the developing world: obtaining clean, safe water; protecting the environment from overuse of resources; adopting more efficient means of growing crops; redefining women's roles; addressing health issues, especially HIV/AIDS; and learning technological skills.

In printed and online books as well as in videos, and on a newly redesigned website (www.peacecorps.gov/wws), the program offers a large number of first-person accounts from Peace Corps volunteers. Most of the stories are accompanied by teaching suggestions or full-fledged lessons. Schools throughout the country are using these materials in language and social studies, geography, art, science, and even math classes. A feature of the web-based offerings is a series of podcasts in which Peace Corps volunteers read their own stories, which web visitors can listen to and download. The program has also posted a series of slide shows in which Peace Corps volunteers narrate illustrated presentations about their experiences abroad. The presentation on Uzbekistan is provided in both English and Spanish. I have my own slideshow online at this site, showing what it was like to live for two years in Saiama. A monthly e-newsletter delivers theme-related teaching ideas and links.

All of the World Wise Schools materials are free. The accompanying lessons help teachers incorporate the materials in existing curricular plans.

Though many Peace Corps volunteers go to the quintessential remote hamlet, many of the 200,000 volunteers to date have lived and worked in urban areas. From the high-rises of Bulgaria and Kazakhstan and Ukraine to single-story homes in rural Paraguay and Ghana, volunteers of all ages are experiencing the shock, the challenge, and the thrill of cross-cultural adjustment.

Thousands of returned Peace Corps volunteers harbor a sense of belonging to an adoptive culture—a sentiment, I can attest, that simply does not fade, even over the course of decades. What one learns about the world by understanding another culture adds immeasurably to the capacity to interact constructively with others—in the classroom, the community, the state, the region, the world.

As challenging as it was to live so culturally isolated in a remote village for close to two years, I wouldn't trade that experience for anything else—then or since.

# IV

# Northern Region

## 13.

### Alone on the Rokel

*Tom Cook*

I wanted to go to Africa for many reasons. Idealism and religion played roles in my choice, as did years of watching Bwana Devil and Tarzan and reading *National Geographic* and even Rudyard Kipling. But my main reason was the pure romantic adventure of it all. I thought it was my generation's opportunity equivalent to World War II. The Peace Corps was the big show. It would be truly something to tell the kids about. Africa was the wild and beautiful land that we would explore and change. I was off to Africa to teach and learn and grow and then fly to Europe to chill for a while. It seemed like a good plan. And it was.

I was uniquely unprepared for life in Africa. I was an idealistic English major from New York City. I lived in an apartment building and had never planted or cared for even a potted house plant. Nor had I ever owned a car or taken a shop course. I was offered a P.C. teaching slot in Ethiopia but could not make the starting date. Fearing the draft, I asked for any other African program. Sierra Leone Community

Development sounded wonderful. Only my *Encyclopedia Britannica* gave me pause. It began by noting that Sierra Leone was often referred to as "the white man's grave."

I loved our training program at Hampton Institute and later, in St. Croix. Everything was new to me. Carpentry, masonry, bridge-building, farming, and language training all presented new challenges for this city guy. I was not very good in any of these pursuits, but I did try hard. Once in St. Croix I was assigned the task of turning large rocks into small rocks for the concrete foundation of one of the new living quarters that we were constructing. This was not a very complicated task. Basically, I would go out into the bush with a pickup truck, collect as many rocks as I could find and then beat them with a sledge hammer until they were much smaller. This was a job that I could understand. No training was necessary. After I finished preparing the foundation for one building, I was congratulated for my work and assigned another floor to prepare. Rather regretfully, I had become a kind of specialist.

Another aspect of training that I loved was the camaraderie that developed among our Peace Corps group. I can still hear some of the songs we sang at night, can taste the beef jerky and beer sold in the local bar, and the burgers with mayo sold in the campus center. I remember how upset we all became when some of our favorite trainees were "de-selected." I still smile at the somewhat obscene and juvenile twists we would add to our Temne instructions, such as *E ba a bana banana*, "I have a big banana." I always though it odd that the Peace Corps would create this highly effective and motivated group of volunteers, and then, once in-country, separate them all and let them fend for themselves. Losing the protective cocoon of the training group was a true shock to my system.

Culture shock did not hit all at once; rather it gradually grew and grew. First upon landing in Dakar, I saw the buzzards waiting on tin-roofed shacks. Then there were the soldiers with automatic weapons surrounding us in Conakry. The ride to Fourah Bay College was an education in itself, with the ferry ride, and the bus ride through Freetown, with all its color and squalor. On the first day, several of our more immature volunteers, myself included, ventured down to Freetown and made a purposeful stop above a forgotten stream watching the local ladies bathe. But this was just fun touring compared with life in our villages.

Things got more serious as we moved upcountry. I remember the volunteers whom we were replacing in Port Loco. They had gaunt faces and seemed burned out by their experiences. They were rough and ready cowboy types who were both admirable and intimidating.

I was assigned to Masimera with my partner, Len Aitken. Len and I were teamed up because Len was highly skilled in many of the technical areas in which I was not. I had and still have deep respect for Len. He was a former member of the U.S. Ski team, confident and competent. Above all, he was a very nice guy. The only problem we ever had was that I sometimes could become jealous of his effectiveness and achievements. Often the local Temne tribesmen would seem to ignore me and instead address Len. Many would ask if I was his son! I was a bit too immature to deal with these issues, but I was always appreciative of his talents.

Our first project in Masimera was perfect for us. The local water supply was a muddy swamp. It smelled horrible, and tasted worse, even after boiling and filtering. The water clogged our filter and we could not produce enough clean drinking water to satiate our daily thirst. The only other source of water available to us was from the Rokel River, about a mile away. We soon began to drive to the Rokel to fill up our containers with river water, which was relatively clean. The Temnes soon were aware of this new water supply. Our landlady requested a share and also a spot in our fridge to keep the water cool. The school teacher and others also requested shares. We began to spend a lot of time fetching river water.

There was one other possible water source in town. A couple of years earlier, a Peace Corps group had dug a well and installed a pump. Unfortunately, the pump handle had broken soon after installation, so the well was inoperative. We decided to repair the handle, and so create a safe and plentiful local water supply. We crossed the river and visited the bauxite mine in Lunsar. Len persuaded a welder to repair the pump handle. The welder said he would do it once only. We returned to Masimera and repaired the pump. The town folk thanked us. Two days later, the handle broke again.

We repeated this process, only to find that the handle was broken once again soon after the second repair. Then we began to see that culture and values played a huge role in this process. We noticed that only the small children drew water. They had moved a large rock next to the pump handle, and would leap from the rock onto the pump handle to create a strong downward stroke. This action, repeated hundreds of times during the course of a day, quickly destroyed the cast iron pump handle. We asked the local headman and the chief to request that only adults or big children use the pump. They would smile as if to say, "That is not how we do things here." I believe we fixed the handle one more time, with similar results. Then we gave up. Africa was not going to change easily.

I suffered from major culture shock those first few months in Sierra Leone. Things like green mambas, rats in the house, no escape from our village (the ferry shut down at dusk), children at our windows morning, noon, and night, no beer, no decent food, and driver ants all conspired to make me ponder what I was doing in Sierra Leone. I managed to lose 30 pounds in the first three months in-country. I am sure many others in our group had similar experiences.

Gradually I became more confident about my surroundings and mission. I never became very good at construction or farming, but I tried. Len led the big projects such as road construction, and making our house livable by building a concrete latrine and a rainwater supply. I was able to organize a football (soccer) team. We cleared a football field, and we had a big game with another village. I played goalie.

After three months or so we were more than ready to visit Freetown for a few days. Freetown kept me going throughout my time in Sierra Leone. Freetown had beaches, beer, movies, hamburgers, hummus, and other volunteers. You could find fresh fish, Gouda cheese, canned milk, Indian restaurants, and fresh bread. The PC hostel had a TV, and except for the voracious bed bugs, it seemed almost like home.

I became very comfortable in Freetown, to an almost dangerous degree. I thought very little of walking alone at night around the more touristy parts of the city. Once after a fine Indian dinner and several Star beers, I walked over to the slave steps, as I believe they were called, leading down to the wharf. I walked down several steps and many people passed by me, no doubt wondering what a *Poto* was doing there at that time of night. Suddenly a man shoved his hand in my rear pocket after my wallet. Fortunately, he grabbed my Barclays Bank book instead. I decided to get the hell out of there with minimal losses incurred. Unfortunately, Barclays made me wait three months before I could use the account again. Each month I had to travel into Freetown just to get my pay.

The beaches near Freetown were lovely. I loved the relatively desolate areas where the mountains seemed to come right down to the sea. I remember swimming at night and diving under the waves only to see the tiny sparks of light made by the phosphorescent microorganisms living in the tropical sea.

One amusing memory involves Mike Leckie. I was having a beer at some forgotten beach bar in the early evening when I noticed Mike enter the bar. We were good friends in training but had not seen each other very often since we arrived in Sierra Leone. He appeared to be carrying some object in one of his hands. On closer inspection, it turned out to be a baby chimp! The animal was holding tightly to Mike's hand, while at the same time it was curled up in a tight ball.

Mike saw me and hurried up to greet me. He said that he had left his wallet in the truck, and requested that I hold the chimp until he returned. I obliged, and Mike set off to his vehicle, which evidently was parked quite a distance away. Suddenly, the chimp became restive, and sensing that I was not his owner, began to give me very nasty looks and sounds. He had a very strong grip for an infant and began to nibble on my hand. I stood on the dance floor of this beach bar, with a scared and angry chimp dangling from my hand, having absolutely no idea of what to do. Eventually Mike returned and retrieved his pet.

After six months or so in Masimera, our boss in Freetown began to urge me to move to another town. He felt that I was ready to try living on my own. He suggested several villages that I could consider. I chose the quaint village of Rokel, on the banks of the wild Rokel River.

My biggest challenge in Rokel was dealing with my near complete isolation. Rokel was one of the more picturesque spots I had visited in Africa. Nestled on the banks of the Rokel River, just below the rapids, it was at the highest navigable point on the river. The town had once been a significant commercial link with the interior of the region before the advent of decent roads. When I arrived, I found rusting tin skeletons of old shops and small warehouses, as well as an old concrete dock. Launches still visited Rokel on rare occasions, but the town obviously was slowly dying.

There were no roads into or out of Rokel. The only way to visit the town was by crossing the river in a dugout canoe. However, the main road to Freetown was only a few miles' walk from the river crossing. There were no shops to speak of in Rokel, although one place did sell hardtack and sardines. Although a few Europeans or Syrians had lived there years before, no one seemed to remember them. Only one person in the town spoke English (the school teacher, of course), and few knew Krio. I spoke Temne, badly, almost entirely during my days there.

Food and water were almost constant problems. I bought many supplies during my monthly visits to Freetown. But I was limited by what I could carry in on my back. I learned to bargain for local treats such as eggs, watermelon, bananas, cucumbers, bush meat (usually duiker), and the occasional pineapple. But there never seemed to be enough food, and I was always hungry. My landlady cooked *chop* for me from time to time, but I never learned to enjoy dried fish. I even settled for hardtack and sardines a few times. That was dietary rock bottom. I managed to develop serious signs of malnutrition, such as stomach pains and boils.

I did not have a fridge for the first six months that I spent in Rokel. It became a challenge to preserve even the hardiest foods from one day to the next. Food spoiled quickly, but ants were the main problem. A tribe of very tiny ants took up residence in my kitchen area. These insects would find my opened tin of Kraft cheese in about two hours, maximum. I cleverly devised a system of placing the open tin in a bowl of water, thus creating a watery moat surrounding the cheese. But the ants also were inventive. These tiny red devils would form a bridge built of their own kind and so cross any watery moat that I devised.

Water was scarce even though I lived on the banks of a beautiful river. Hauling water was no fun for me or for my houseboy. I owned only two buckets; one I used for drinking water and one for bathing. Every night I would stand on my back steps and shower in the dark with the aid of a tin can punctured with holes. During the day I would often watch the Temnes bathing in the river and enjoying themselves. Always hot and smelly, I envied their freedom to ignore Peace Corps medical advice and just dive into our wonderful, cool, bacterial rich, hookworm-infested river. Finally, after a few months, I succumbed to the temptation, a true guilty pleasure. I loved swimming in that river, never saw a crocodile, and only got hookworms twice.

Rokel had lots of wildlife, particularly snakes. We had mambas, boomslangs, night adders, Gabon vipers and, of course, spitting cobras. At dusk, I would often watch the cobras swimming across the Rokel. The Temnes thought it odd that I wanted to examine captured snakes to identify their species. I used to come upon adders on the trails around the village, and would use a stick to extend their fangs to identify them as poisonous. Once, my houseboy killed a spitting cobra that wandered into my bedroom.

I tried several different projects in Rokel, which achieved varying degrees of success. I started another football club, and cleared another field for play. The football talent in Rokel was considerably better than in Masimera, so my success as goalkeeper suffered greatly. I began an adult literacy program that met four or five times before dying of members' boredom and unrealistic expectations. I created upland rice seed demonstration plots and successfully sold fertilizer to several of the local farmers. I begged land from the local chief and grew bananas and cucumbers for my own consumption. I reluctantly researched and planned a large 60-foot bridge across a tributary of the Rokel. I sincerely doubted my ability to construct such a large bridge over a rapidly flowing river spanning such a large distance. Fortunately, this project was awarded to a government contractor.

Entertainment in Rokel was practically nonexistent. I had neither radio nor record player. The local "Jolly Society" would serenade for a shilling when I had the cash. The youths would play their instruments and dance on my front porch. Most days, I would entertain myself with reading and writing a diary. There was a small shop across the river that stocked Guinness stout, which the locals considered to be a medicine, thanks the ubiquitous signs stating, "Guinness is good for you!" Most evenings I would need a little medical care, and would send my houseboy across the river for two bottles of warm stout. Life had its compensations.

After many months of isolation, I became somewhat desperate for companionship. Once to my amazement I saw a white man paddling a kayak pass by my window. I could not believe my eyes. I ran down to the dock and yelled to him. He was an English diplomat on an exploratory holiday paddle up the mighty Rokel. I showed him the town, and invited him to lunch. We shared some water, hardtack, and sardines, and he took my picture, and later mailed the prints to me. He said that I reminded him of Robinson Crusoe. That was a big day in Rokel.

Another time after one of my more and more frequent jaunts into Freetown, I arrived late in the afternoon at the canoe launch. An old lady was waiting to cross, but the ferry man was nowhere to be seen. Foolishly, I began to ferry the lady and myself across the rain-swollen Rokel. I took the canoe upstream along the river edge several hundred yards above my landing point, and then swung the canoe out into the center of the swift and turbulent river. We made good progress toward the far bank, and finally came to a few yards of the landing. Unfortunately, I was spent. We slid past the landing, and brushing the mangroves, we rapidly continued down river. My companion began to shriek and call out for help. Most of the town rushed down to the river and then ran after us downstream. The lady frantically tried to grab passing branches and trees, which probably would have resulted in capsizing the canoe and throwing us both in the river. Eventually, I was able to paddle the last few yards to the shore. I wound up at least a quarter of a mile below the landing. Walking back to town with most of the population chattering around me, I was glad that my Temne was not good enough to understand their comments.

Succeed or fail, win or lose, I look back with pride at my time in Rokel. That I was able to survive and adapt in such isolated and primitive conditions for almost 14 months seems an accomplishment in its own right. Living without even basic necessities such as a fridge, vehicle, decent food, or English-speaking companionship would not be possible for me now. I just could not do it.

I still dream of returning to Rokel, in spite of the ravages that the civil war evidently inflicted on the town and region. Some of my dreams are fun and wistful, like swimming in the river with the young women. Some are dark and lonely. The dark dreams often involve walking down the two-mile road from the lorry stop to the canoe launch. I hear the birds crying and the monkeys screaming. The dark tree limbs block out most of the sun, but it is very warm. I walk down the hill to the river, and the tree canopy gradually snuffs out all of the sunlight. The pungent smell of cooking fires fills the air. The river is swift and dark, laterite red. No ferry man is present. I cross the river to rusting Rokel, and I am scared and all alone.

Toward the end of my time in Sierra Leone my boss asked me to help out with an in-country training program for new volunteers. The program was to be run around the Port Loco area. I helped with the construction of a school building in some remote town. One of my main functions was to bring construction supplies to the site. On one occasion, I was bringing a load of cement to our work site. My heavily laden Land Rover split the palm log bridge, and the rear two wheels were left dangling above the water. We were next to a herd of wild-acting African cattle, and two bulls fought near our vehicle. Somehow my companion and I were able to lever up the rear wheels and drive out of this precarious situation.

Another time, after working for most of the day on the building, it became apparent that we were running short of some construction items. I grabbed one of the few trucks available and headed to Free-town as dusk descended. After proceeding 30 or so miles down the road in the dark, I heard a loud noise and could see sparks from my truck in my rear view mirror. I stopped and looked for a flashlight in the glove box. No such luck. I could tell that something was dragging from the vehicle. I parked next to a small village in the middle of nowhere. The town was having some sort of celebration, with much singing and yelling. Frankly, it was a lonely and scary situation. Suddenly a lorry appeared out of the dark and stopped at my vehicle. The Temne-speaking gentleman offered to help and had a flashlight. I borrowed his light and crawled under the truck. I found that one end of the drive shaft to the front wheels had fallen off. I was about to panic at the prospects of sleeping on the road, when I realized that I could simply remove the other end of the shaft and drive off.

Even now I feel that this moment was symbolic of my growth and maturation in the Peace Corps. I cannot imagine even trying to accomplish such a procedure before my time in Africa. Roadside car repair in the dark, with only a flashlight and a wrench, broke new ground for my self-confidence.

Time seemed to move fast after I left Sierra Leone. I spent four of the happiest months of my life drifting around Morocco and Western Europe. I arrived home just after Christmas in 1967 and just before the Tet Offensive in Vietnam. I married my first wife in mid-March 1968, and was drafted into the U.S. Army by early June, the day of Robert Kennedy's funeral. One year after leaving Sierra Leone, I found myself graduating from Basic Training at Fort Gordon, Georgia. Talk about culture shock! The year before I was trying to help poor peasants and now I was training to kill poor peasants. Fortunately I never had to serve in Vietnam. This was beyond ironic. I remember wondering to myself, what happened? Where did everyone go? What is the point of all this? I am not sure that I ever answered those questions. But I tried and I survived.

# 14.
## Building a Bridge in Masimera

*Len Aitken*

I have fond memories of arriving at Hampton Institute and joining what I thought was a fun-loving group of eccentric characters to do rural development in Sierra Leone. These were exciting times. What did we know about rural development? Most of us were fresh out of college and social activists. Change was sweeping our country, and many of us had been involved with the civil rights and Vietnam War movements at our respective colleges. Friendships formed easily and beer seemed to flow readily.

What initially stood out was how many in our group were deeply involved with music. Many played instruments, and others were incredible vocalists. The ring leaders—Gerry Cashion, Hugh McAllorum, and Janet Horton— knew the words to hundreds of songs. At the end of several tunes, Cashion would grab his Adam's apple between his thumb and forefinger and twitch it to create a warble effect in his voice. But beyond my appreciation for Cashion's special effects, I loved the music. It was heartfelt and joyful, and it spoke to me in a way that was strangely foreign. I had no musical background and little talent. At an early age I was dismissed from the choir at St. John's Church because of my inclination to hum the vocals. No one had ever before been asked to leave the choir. My dismissal was unsettling and left me questioning my musical abilities. How would I, tone deaf, fit in with this Peace Corps group? I began by humming, and with enough alcohol, my voice gained strength. I remember the liberating feeling of knowing that no matter how off key or loud I was, nobody gave a damn. By the time we hit the Virgin Islands, I was a singer. I loved the warm tropical air, white beaches, snorkeling, and evenings of beer and music. I knew the Peace Corps was for me.

When the door to the plane opened, we were hit by a blast of steaming hot humid air that immediately filled the cabin. With it came the smell of rotting garbage, baked urine, and fumes from the plane's engine. Welcome to Sierra Leone. A wave of nausea swept over me. It was an "Oh shit" moment. Within seconds I was drenched with sweat. Two years of this? I was in full panic. In the time it took the ramp wranglers to hitch up to the plane, I had conjured up 10 solid reasons why I needed to leave Sierra Leone and seek reassignment elsewhere. What about Tibet or Peru? I had always seen myself as tough and emotionally stable, but here I was, homesick nauseated, and my feet hadn't even hit the tarmac. As we exited the plane, I looked at the others for signs of distress. There were none. Couples were holding hands and laughing!

I was assigned to Masimera, a small town that was the headquarters of a chiefdom of the same name, in the Port Loko District. Masimera consisted of about 10 huts and was located about six miles southeast of Lunsar, the largest town in the district. My housemate was Tom Cook. On our first morning, we threw open the shutters to find a crowd of 20 or 30 villagers at the window, hungry for a glimpse of the white boys waking up. It was another "Oh shit" moment, as though we were the main attraction in a zoo. I stumbled outside and desperately positioned myself in front of the hole that was to be our toilet. As I urinated, my audience erupted with laughs, shouts, and applause for my performance. From my limited Temne language skills, I could understand that they were excited to see that all my body parts were white. I quickly retreated inside where Tom, obviously paralyzed by the thought of "life in captivity" was desperately sucking on his third cigarette of the morning. In time, the novelty of the "two white guys" wore off. We built walls around the hole in the ground for a bit of privacy, and one monotonous day folded into the next.

Our chief, Bia Koblo, was an affable guy who had spent some time at school in England and who owned a stable of wives. He funded our first project, a 10-foot-long bridge over a creek. I assembled a work crew of 15 men, and we dug the foundations. One man, Kabu, selected himself to be the head of the crew, which meant that he would do nothing except give orders. Guided by my Peace Corps-driven desire to undo years of white supremacy, I grabbed a shovel on the first day and pitched in. I was here to project a new image of the "white man," a guy who got his hands dirty and worked alongside his black brothers. My workers laughed at my efforts and insisted that I be the "big man." They seemed to take pride in knowing that if they were working on a job for a white man, the job must be very important. So much for meddling with the image of the "white man."

Meanwhile, I went to Lunsar to shop for cement. I was determined not to get sucked into the system of bribery that we had been warned about in training. Chief Bia Koblo steered me to a Lebanese shop where the owner plied me with beer and several hours of small talk about life in Lebanon. We struck a deal that he would truck the cement to the jobsite for free and would then "invoice the District later because that's the way he and the chief always did it." The price of the cement? I never knew. Welcome to "Business as We Do It 101."

Sand was available, but we needed aggregate. Not to worry. Kabu and his men gathered up large rocks, and using hammers they broke the rocks into three-quarter-inch aggregate. Every day the 14 men would produce one-quarter yard of aggregate. We needed about 15 yards total. To keep spirits up and the men on task, Kabu asked that we hire a drummer. The next day a drummer arrived with two assistant drummers. They drummed right into the rainy season, when the project was temporarily abandoned due to "cold temperatures."

A year into our service, I woke up one morning wildly sick. My trips to the outhouse grew more frequent as the day progressed. By late afternoon I was slightly delusional, confused, and I found myself talking out loud incessantly. Was this dysentery or malaria or a combination? This was an authentic "Oh shit" moment. I took every medicine that I could find in our kit and decided to tough it out for the night. Tom Cook had moved to another village, so I no longer had a housemate. In the morning I awoke and stumbled to the Land Rover. I realized I was more than slightly delusional when I had trouble finding the road out of town. There was only one road out of town. The next problem was finding Tom Cook's village. Somehow I did find Tom, probably because he was sitting outside his house as I drove by. Tom took the wheel and armed with two rolls of toilet paper, we headed for Freetown. His only request was that I stop talking. Tom was great, allowing "courtesy stops" every so often so that I could make a dash into the bush. Finally we reached Freetown, the Peace Corps rest house, and the doctor. Within five days, I was again able to drink beer, the barometer of good health.

Living next door to people, I got to see a good deal of daily life. There were arguments, wife beatings, sick people, and funerals, but generally people were happy and went about life in good spirits. Language was always a barrier to understanding what was going on. For information, I relied on the only English-speaker in town, Fodi, who split his time between being the teacher and the town drunk. Although Fodi was a Mende, he had been assigned by the Catholic church to teach in our Temne town. He resented being assigned to a Temne village and had few kind words to say about the Temnes. The pejorative he used to describe them was "primitive." In his sober moments, Fodi offered interesting insights into the culture. Our village was Muslim except on Friday, when the church brought out free food for all the Catholics.

As is the Muslim tradition, men, especially chiefs, took several wives. One day a boy, who looked to be about 16, was brought to trial for "woman damage." Evidently he had slept with one of the local chief's younger wives. When I asked Fodi why the chief's little wife had ratted on the boy, he lapsed into a complex discussion, explaining that by ratting on the boy, the boy would be punished by having to work on the chief's farm for two years. But the chief was then obligated to house, feed, and care for the boy. Interestingly, there were no hard feelings about the affair. Since the chief now had another laborer, he could plant a bigger farm and earn more money. And with that money he might buy another wife. Was there ever a concern that the boy might have impregnated the girl in question? "No," Fodi said, "We don't worry about that because all babies are welcome. If the baby is a boy he will be a good farm worker, and if it is a girl she will bring a bride price." It struck me that this was a very complete economic and social welfare system that had been developed and refined over centuries. Teenagers learn about sex, pay the price, and learn agricultural skills. The local economy benefits with more agricultural produce, the elderly are respected and cared for, and women are housed, fed, and cared for by their husband. I concede there are shortcomings, but what system is perfect?

During slow times, I would go with Tom to Ed Ebel's place in Port Loko. It was a headquarters and a gathering place for Peace Corps volunteers throughout the northern region. We all liked it because the house came with a cook. In the evenings, we would often find ourselves at a nearby open air bar. One day an elderly lady stopped by our table offering to sell oranges. When we declined, she started yelling at us. We had no idea why. Then for reasons we never understood, she took one of her breasts, which was very flat and very long, and flipped it up onto her shoulder, where it remained. The guys went wild. When she repeated the trick with her other breast, we emptied our wallets. You'll never see this in Las Vegas. This had come to be our idea of a good time. Needless to say, the lady reappeared whenever we were at the bar.

When the dry season came around, work on the bridge began again. On average we worked only two or three days a week because the men had to tend their farms, and they needed days off for Muslim holidays. After several more months of work, the bridge was finished and backfilled with dirt. This was the only project I completed in the time I was in Sierra Leone. To celebrate the completion of the bridge, we invited to the grand opening ceremony Chief Bia Koblo, district officials, some Catholic priests, a witch doctor, a lorry driver, and, of course, the locals. The only people who showed up were the locals, the witch doctor, and a lorry driver. Before the driver would drive over the bridge with his lorry filled with passengers, he wanted the witch doctor to declare the bridge safe and free from devils. The witch doctor, an ordinary guy in khaki pants, unceremoniously appeared out of the woods with a stick that had a smoldering ball at one end. He proceeded to pray aloud as he walked over and under the bridge for about 10 minutes with his smoking stick. He then stopped and proclaimed to the crowd that the bridge was not safe to drive over. Everyone accepted what he said without question, and without any outward signs of disappointment they all went home. When I asked Fodi what had transpired, he simply said that these Temne people are very primitive and they believe the bridge has devils in it. Presumably, the witch doctor would be able to un-devil the bridge on a second try. It was obviously a pay-for-pray operation. I never saw a lorry pass over the bridge before I left Sierra Leone, two weeks later.

Since leaving Sierra Leone, I have run into only one Sierra Leonean. Five years ago I was skiing cross-country in the Colorado Rockies when I came upon a black couple also enjoying a day of sunshine and fresh snow. We were all stopped at the top of a hill when I struck up a conversation. Imagine my surprise when the man said he was from Sierra Leone. Immediately I burst into my Krio and threw in a bit of Temne to impress him. He was stunned and delighted. Here he was standing at 9,500 feet surrounded by mountain peaks 13,000 feet high and a stranger comes up to him out of nowhere and starts speaking in his native tongue. His wife, a good natured American, loved it. The three of us formed a brief but unforgettable bond as we skied together for two more hours speaking Krio and remembering past times in Sierra Leone.

I've been a filmmaker for the past 40 years. A year ago I produced a film on building with adobe with a New Mexico man, Quentin Wilson. In the course of looking at and talking about earth as being possibly the most energy efficient and sustainable building material of the future, he showed us pictures of "wattle and daub," which he described as "an ancient building technique" using mud packed around interwoven sticks like bamboo to create walls. That describes the way every house in Masimera was built. I never knew it was a traditional art.

# 15.

# Beginning Marriage in Peace Corps Service

*Charles and Moira Geoffrion*

M uch in love, we were walking hand-in-hand in an early evening through Kendall Square in Boston. A motorcycle escort entered the square. It was soon followed by an open limo in which John and Jacqueline Kennedy sat waving to us and the many others who cheered them from just a few feet away. The motorcade passed slowly, in an age of hope and innocence, absent today's layers of security. Perhaps it was that moment that solidified our resolve to volunteer and to answer the call to service to America by committing two years of work in an emerging nation. Suburbia could wait.

We asked to be assigned to Francophone Africa, but the only program opening at the time was for Sierra Leone, a newly independent former British colony. We accepted.

## Program and Training

In 1965, its fifth year of operation, the Peace Corps was looking specifically for married couples to commit to work in remote areas, as an alternative to the earlier days, when single men were given pickup trucks and built bridges, schools, and clinics, and single women lived and taught on school compounds. Our program was called Community Development. It required a well screened personality test to ensure that those selected to live in such remote areas could handle the isolation. Emphasis was on the study of the local language and the area's history and culture. We were not nurses or engineers; we were "B.A. Generalists" with a desire to work in a vaguely defined program still in its formative phase.

We were fortunate to arrive at Hampton Institute for training at a time when the available dormitory rooms were assigned to others. Nearly all the other trainees were in the "Wigwam" building, a structure that had once been the residence of Native American students on this otherwise all-black campus where Indians, too, were segregated. This was fortunate because we were assigned to live off-campus in the home of the school's Post Mistress. Mrs. Young eagerly took us and another Peace Corps trainee couple in as family. Having her support and friendship, along with fresh baked biscuits every morning, made the 11-week training program all the more meaningful.

We tended to stay on the Hampton Institute campus, a beautiful coastal setting, since our radical and racially mixed group was treated poorly by most of the local folks. Many local merchants proudly proclaimed, "We have to serve 'them' but we don't have to serve you!" This tension only worsened when Charles and fellow trainee Steve Bingham began spending their free time working with a local attorney to force the integration of the local hospital based on the new Civil Rights Act of 1964.

The highlight of the training was the interaction we all had with our language teachers. Charles and Moira were assigned to learn Temne, one of the dozen or so languages spoken in Sierra Leone. This was our first contact with Sierra Leoneans, and we made fast friendships with Seltzer Kante Morgan and Ibrahim Kamara, both graduate students studying in the USA and hired to help with language and cultural understanding. Since Temne was not a written language, we had daily mimeographed study sheets and lots of *in situ* conversational exercises. We met a minimum of six hours a day for language learning.

Our training program ended with five weeks at the Peace Corps's U.S. Virgin Island Training Center in St. Croix. There we had our first experience of village life, when a portion of our group was assigned to the area known euphemistically as "Profit." It was an impoverished area where we worked diligently to complete a clinic that had been begun by another Peace Corps group in training.

Since the program on St. Croix was designed as an outward bound experience, the training staff often thought up ways to try our patience or push our resolve as preparation for the real life living we were about to confront when in West Africa. One evening we were all invited for a group dinner at the training headquarters, and it "happened" that the van to return us to our assigned villages was not available.

There was no moon that night when, well after dark, we set off to walk the three or four miles back to where we were assigned. In between passing cloud cover, the star light illuminated the way along dirt roads of no traffic to speak of. Seeing the edge of the roadway was possible only by looking at stars above us. This gave us the needed guidance along the roads that were otherwise lined with tall trees and heavy brush overgrowth. Seeing the dim distant lantern lights and hearing barking dogs from Profit were a true welcome that night. Now we knew we could "handle" Africa.

## Heading Upcountry, At Last

One of the Peace Corps volunteers working the Port Loko district took us in his Chevy pickup, loaded with our furniture, to Mange-Bureh Chiefdom. Just a half mile before arriving at the village, however, we encountered what became a major feature in our lives for the next two years: the Little Scarsies River. To get across this body of water, we drove down a steep embankment to a waiting barge. It was connected by two vertical side posts via wooden pulleys to a cable that ran across the 150-yard crossing. We carefully drove onto the floating wooden platform.

Then it began. Two workers poled us away from shore and began walking along the edge of the ferry pulling on two wooden mallets, each with notches that grabbed the cable. Their effort forced the ferry slowly away from shore and across to the other side. During the rainy season, as the level of the river water increased, the force of water flowing past the barge made it easier for the workers, who no longer had to pull so hard. The current pushed the ferry across. The more water there was, the less work was needed. However, there came a point when the water got so high that the ferry became unstable. The barge moved fast across to the waiting shore where it slammed into the waiting roadway.

The river now behind us, we climbed the northern embankment and made the turn into the center of Mange-Bureh, where we were met by the paramount chief and his family, along with other village leaders, including Mr. Kanu, the native administration clerk. Most importantly, we met Pa Alimamy Yeli, the brother of the chief's first wife. He had prepared a home for us and took us in as family for our entire stay.

## Village Life

During the first hour of introductions and chaos, as the entire village turned out to meet us, we could not help but notice one older, short man who kept moving to stand behind Charles. As the furniture (bed, table, two chairs, a small kerosene refrigerator and stove, and a couple of lanterns) was moved into the mud house, we learned that a pit latrine had been built in the back. Suddenly the older man was gone. We soon found him working in the latrine, busily sawing an opening in the bottom of a wooden crate which, when inverted, became a toilet seat over the pit. He was the village carpenter, assigned to this duty. His estimate was quite accurate, and the opening fit Charles perfectly, but it was never quite right for Moira.

Suddenly we both realized that we were "on our own" with no electricity, no running water, no telephone or television. The first order of work was to set up the mosquito net above the bed and to arrange our "C" rations, a few cases of which were left along with our luggage and furniture. There were no glass windows in the house, but the window openings were secured by wooden shutters, which we closed for that first night. Exhausted, we retreated under the net shortly after dark. Charles turned on his portable shortwave radio and searched for a BBC or Voice of America broadcast, desperate to feel some sense of connection with the world left behind. Later that first night, we were awakened by drumming and singing not far from our hut, just below us in a dry area that would flood dramatically during the rains. We loved the rhythmic beating, chanting, and clapping. This was the "real" Africa we had studied about. And, within the hour we learned just how real that was.

A divided world of cultures expressed itself in the form of sudden and painful screaming as the drumming heightened to a near frenzy. We later learned that clitoridectomy was being performed in a traditional coming-of-age ceremony for some village young women. Reading about such an abstract concept seemed a titillating exercise in anthropology. Hearing these girls' penetrating, wailing cries rendered any abstract notion as useless tools of understanding.

Dawn broke, but we slept. When we stirred, we were met with small, gentle sounds of even younger children. We soon realized that they had been waiting for us to get up. It must have been two or three hours into daylight. Were we dead in there? We looked toward the shutters, and through the knots and key holes we saw looking back at us the eyes of village children of all ages, curious and hopeful, wondering what we were all about.

## Finding Our Roles

Thus began a regime that would continue daily throughout our many months among the Temne people. Light the kerosene stove, get some water boiling, make the coffee, open the doors and windows, and, most importantly, with a cheerful *"n' diari, n' diari noi,"* greet the many villagers who had gathered to wish us well.

From the beginning, they came with sick children hoping we could provide medicine. Although our assignment was vaguely described as "community development" aimed mostly toward nutrition and agricultural improvement, we quickly recognized that basic medical attention was essential. Most of the children had tropical ulcerations. Common flies were so ubiquitous that any cut or scrape drew dozens of them to the wound site, soon followed by deep infection. It was basic hygiene: remove the puss and scabbing, clean the wound with Detol, a disinfectant, and apply often out-of-date antibiotic ointment, then cover with clean, dry bandages. It was most rewarding when, a week or so later, the first children approached, often with their family, to thank us for successfully healing their wounds.

Moira went about setting up a nutrition program that she determined, along with several village women, would best be managed by hosting a daily distribution of basic meals based on bulgar and cooking oil. CARE and Catholic Relief Services administered the bulk food stores in the capital city and provided us with 60-pound burlap bags of this wheat grain, along with five- gallon tins of cooking oil.

Moira's women's local leadership committee decided to charge a penny per large bowl of food, available only to children five years and younger and pregnant women. The small revenue provided just enough to pay a cook and to purchase some green vegetables or sometimes a fish to add to the pot. Meanwhile, Charles was off doing "men's things," mostly sitting at the chief's council and listening to village management issues being debated.

Once we established a routine and our language skills improved, there was delight in being somewhat successful on bridging the cultural divide. The relative hardship of living without modern conveniences was less of a challenge than fully understanding the nuances of local issues. Trying to avoid doing something really stupid was a daily goal. For example, if Charles was walking to a village he had heard about on the periphery of the chiefdom, and he stopped to ask someone how much farther he had to walk, the answer inevitably came "It is far small," meaning it is not so far. But who was this villager to tell some "Poto," meaning a white man, who was obviously intent on getting somewhere that it is a stupidly long walk on a very hot day, and he doesn't have enough drinking water to get there and return? Returning much later than he had planned that day, thoroughly parched and without water, Charles stopped at a small village opening on the rainforest trail and was immediately welcomed by the village headman, who summoned a small boy and instructed him to climb a tree to cut a coconut. The headman then with great ceremony de-husked it with a large machete and then cut it open at the top, offering Charles the most refreshing drink he ever remembered. It turned out that one of the children Charles and Moira had helped heal lived in this village, and word had spread that *O Peacee Corps* were good people. "Mr. Charley" was getting known around the area.

## Feelings of Isolation

Newly married and feeling every bit as still on an extended honeymoon, we began to realize that we had to be everything to each other. Back home there would be double dates, going to movies and restaurants, ball games, concerts, night clubs. Moira had her girlfriends, and Charles had his buddies, but not here.

It was just the two of us for companionship every day, all day. Yes, there were village friends, but the cultural divide was so profound that it was as if we had arrived in Mange-Bureh on some mystical time machine that deposited them in a past century among people who could not possibly relate to our issues of adjustment in such a foreign surrounding. Take drinking water; hydration was essential. The local water was polluted. Looking upstream one day from the river bank where people took their water, Charles photographed a typical scene. There were cows wading in the shallow area, women bathing and doing laundry, children urinating, and, while unknown to locals, he knew of the numerous waterborne micro-organisms that caused a variety of tropical diseases. Charles began a daily process of boiling two or three gallons and then filtering it through ceramic candle filters. It took all day for the filtration, so today's water preparation was for use tomorrow. Miss a day and you were left with drinking super-sweet Vimto or some other version of 7-Up.

One night a loud banging on the door woke us. In desperation, a mother held a baby who was clearly suffering from a serious croup. Barely able to breathe, the boy was in a life-threatening condition. Moira immediately yelled for Charles to get some water boiling and made a steam tent from towels. To the amazement of the small crowd that had gathered, she took the little guy, now screaming in terror, away from his mother and under the tent with her. Slowly the warm moisture helped to relax and open the child's airways. The crying stopped and he slept peacefully. From that night on, word spread, and we were now officially in the healthcare business.

The nearby Catholic mission school had a small clinic on its property. About once a month, Dr. Gorgy, an Italian medical doctor and brother of the Xaverian order, would arrive and see people in need of more complicated medical care. This became an obvious link for Charles and Moira to extend the health care efforts needed in the area. Under Dr. Gorgy's tutelage, *O Peacee Corps* got both technical guidance and stock medications beyond the scope of their more basic Red Cross training. As Charles traveled through the outlying villages or Moira identified health needs among her growing feeding program participants, we determined who should be scheduled to see Dr. Gorgy. As time passed, Gorgy, a surgeon, trained Charles to assist, and later they traveled together to remote villages to perform procedures for people incapable of travel.

## Fun and Frustration

We were given two puppies on a day when, as it happened, we were both frustrated about our lack of progress in getting people to think ahead and plan for the future. So we gladly accepted these dogs and named one of them *Tumtumne* (in Temne, "think") and the other *Ta Ninung* (for the future). Months passed and our efforts for planning continued to slip and slide, but the entire village related to our dogs in friendly and positive ways. No one in the village gave names to their dogs, nor did they care for them as we do in America, but everyone in Mange-Bureh Chiefdom knew *Tumtumne* and *Ta Ninung*, calling out to them when they passed by and sometimes offering them a snack. These were not dogs that scavenged through the gutters or fought in the trash piles.

Many months later it was clear that *Ta Ninung* was ill, a sickness that quickly presented as rabies. Charles had to borrow a gun and sadly, shoot him. He shot "the future," and this fact was not unnoticed by the village community. They knew all too well that one cannot truly plan for the future. As subsistence farmers, this was simply impossible. The ever-present forces of nature and the vagaries of local and national politics rendered people in such circumstances helpless to attempt any planning. So much for Peace Corps goals.

Then, there was another kind of "medicine." This time we were not the providers but only picked up the pieces. On a very hot late afternoon, we heard a loud-voiced cursing in a tone of voice that could only be American. Stepping out of their hut, there, just about 50 yards away on the North–South dirt road that ran through the village, was fellow Peace Corps volunteer Bob Galeria. He was one of the single guys with a pickup truck, working in a village about 30 miles to the north in the Bombali District. He had blown a tire, and his spare was also flat. As it became clear, Bob was having a bad day, but he had arrived, by chance and without knowing it, in front of the Geoffrions' place. Charles had raised a tank of water high enough so that with a length of garden hose, he was able to make a shower stall next to the latrine. This was much better than the typical bucket shower. Having a shower along with a home-cooked meal, a haircut from Moira and his clothes laundered in the river, all made Bob a rejuvenated man, ready to get a tire patched and head south the next day.

Moira did much of the cooking, often improvising with a couple of frying pans, one inverted over the other to form a mini oven. Charles handled the routine of cleaning soot off the bottom of the pans from the kerosene stove, preparing the lantern wicks for use when it got dark, or pressurizing the Petromax lantern when we wanted a really bright light. The water filtration ceramic wicks had to be cleaned each evening for use the next day. It all worked well, this "home away from home."

For times when local vegetables, fish, or chicken (always with rice) was not on the menu, we kept a backup supply of canned foods purchased in Freetown. One favorite was the British-made Smedley's beef pie. The tin it came in was the shape of a small pie plate, and Moira kept this tin in the hopes of baking a pie as a surprise for Charles. She had secretly gotten a hold of a can of cherries for this purpose, and kept it well hidden. Using her clever combination of frying pans, one inverted over the other, the pie was in the oven.

Charles returned from a day being away at smaller villages. When he got home, he immediately smelled what he could not believe to be true. Was there a pie baking in that little oven? It was true. Wow! After a shower, he returned to join Moira for a candlelit dinner, and, as he was really hungry, he went back for what remained on the stove. Meanwhile, Moira began to eat some pie. On this occasion they had also opened a bottle of wine, enjoyed only on special times. Moira ate some more pie. In the low light of two candles, and while sharing the tales of the day's activities, neither noticed that Moira had consumed the entire rest of the cherry pie before Charles had finished his second helping. To this day, Charles enjoys reminding Moira of that evening.

But then, Moira has her own story to tell. In village culture it is quite common for women to be bare breasted, but always covered from the hips to knees or ankles. Both men and women were often seen bathing naked along streams or rivers. The dark skin of the local people blended into the landscape, all beautifully natural. But once when Charles was bathing in the small shower stall next to the latrine where he had hooked up a green hose that ran from the raised water storage tank and into the thatch roof, he suddenly noticed that there were two "green hoses" and quickly realized that one was a green mamba. Without hesitation and leaving his towel behind, Charles ran out of the shower stall across the yard and right into the middle of a group of women who were sitting with Moira. There was never a better example of how white skin stands out in contrast to nature! Amid raucous laughter, the women put out the alarm, *"o bok, o yi di,"* (there is a snake here), and two men from next door rushed in with machetes to dispatch the creature while Charles made a tactful retreat to his dressing room.

## The Unpredictable Becomes Routine

Moira's work with nutrition evolved into a well-managed routine, and the daily clinical activities were also becoming predictable, with the obvious emergency exceptions. During a hot midafternoon when most people were under shade and waiting for the cooler part of the day to return, three young teenage boys ran to our hut, gasping for breath and in much need of hydration. It was difficult to understand these boys, since they were Susu people from the north and spoke Temne with difficulty. Charles simply knew they needed him to follow them, so grabbing his basic kit, they headed off on foot toward the north. About two hours later, not far from a district dirt road they had been following, they came to the boys' friend. He was propped up against the base of a tree, covered in blood and gasping for breath.

Assessing this young man's condition, it was evident that metal objects were stuck in his chest but fortunately, they were not deeply imbedded. As Charles began to carefully remove each piece he recognized bits of razor blade, nails, screws, and small chunks of iron. The bleeding was contained with compression and a bandage applied. Then the story unfolded. These guys, all brothers, had been hunting monkeys using a "Dane gun." This was a homemade rifle from which fragments of metal were fired, in the absence of real bullets. Who knows where they got the powder charge to fire the device? The boys had forced a large monkey into an isolated tree and it had no escape route to follow. Staying high in the tree, the monkey eluded capture, so one brother climbed to get a better position for a shot. Another brother then passed the rifle up to him, barrel first. It went off, hitting the hunter square in the upper chest.

Since the boy's breathing remained very shallow, Charles was concerned that there may have been lung penetration, so he wanted to get this boy to the regional hospital. Some local villagers began to appear. Nothing happened in these parts that did not spread like a "breaking news" bulletin across the area. Charles was getting worried, thinking of options for transporting the kid when a pickup truck came down the dirt road in a cloud of dry season dust. Of course, the driver stopped as he approached the scene that now included about 20 men, women, and children. They all claimed to know the boys' family and some were beginning to wail in worry that the boy would die. Charles asked if the driver would transport the boy to Port Loko for medical attention. He agreed, and the boy was placed in the empty open back of the pickup and driven off.

## A New Means of Transport: Better than A Bike in the Rains

Hot and lengthy hikes like this got Charles thinking that, with very few roads, a bicycle that barely worked, and the majority of people living close to the Little Scarsies River, would it not be better to extend his outreach by boat? The problem was the few "Pampa Boats" that traveled this river were extremely slow, putting in to every village for hours at a time as goods, animals, and people were transferred off or on.

Since Charles had grown up enjoying boats on Cape Cod, he explored this thinking with Moira. She immediately suggested that her skills as a dress designer could help. "Let's build a full scale pattern out of newspaper and see what it looks like," she said. Thus began the complicated process of building a boat from scratch. The chief provided an old, abandoned mud hut near the river's edge as a workshop, since the rainy season was fast approaching. The local carpenter offered to help and provided a source for the only available wood, mahogany. This boat project actually started to look like it could be done. A trip to Port Loko and the hardware store got the needed supplies. A visit to Peace Corps headquarters led to a link with CARE, which provided a 30 horsepower Evinrude outboard motor. And finally, Charles was able to talk the district commissioner into providing 55-gallon drums of petrol and motor oil as needed. Now to get to work!

The rainy season in Sierra Leone was something to witness. It began slowly with afternoon storms as a tease. But soon they built to massive storm fronts that swept across the area with a deluge. In the preceding months, the heat and humidity had built to nearly intolerable levels. No electricity meant no air conditioning, no fans, and no ice cubes. You just moved around in slow mode, experiencing a miasma of misery. It was not a pleasant time of year.

As the rainy season took hold, the storms grew longer and more numerous. The volume of water falling from the heavily clouded sky was truly impressive. The winds ripped through the area. Pelting drops stung the flesh. Soon the storms blurred into hours of heavy incessant downpour. At night it could be totally distracting, even frightening. After all, when in a structure made from mud and stick with a thatched roof, the sense of stability in a storm is simply lacking; just think of the story of the Three Little Pigs!

From the knowledge gained from geosynchronous weather satellites, we now understand that the many hurricanes that track across the southern Atlantic, west-bound for the Caribbean, the Gulf of Mexico, and Florida are all weather systems that spin off the coast of Sierra Leone. Living through the violence and power of these storms as they battered Mange-Bureh, it is easy to appreciate how a hurricane is born.

It turned out that there was no better time than the rains to build a boat. While Moira's nutrition program continued apace, Charles could no longer venture into the farm fields or nearby villages without serious risk. At the height of the rains, travel needed to be limited to work in the immediate area, so every day Charles and *o ciamder*, the village carpenter, got together and began sawing mahogany and laying out the boat, board and truss by side panel and transom. It was rather like "going to work." Whereas most Peace Corps days were casual and rather unstructured, the boat-building enterprise became a real job. Try hand drilling over 700 holes into hardwood, then soap up two-and-a-half-inch brass screws and hand turn them into place. Wood was shaped, glued, and clamped. Charles learned to "measure twice and cut once."

The boat was almost 20 feet long, with a broad beam, and probably overbuilt, but Charles was worried about plying an unknown and forceful river that was full of boulders and sand bars along with crocodiles and hippos. The interior bow area was used to build in a storage compartment that could be locked. The center part of the boat had collapsible benches that ran lengthwise, not from side to side, so that the boat could more easily carry bags of fertilizer or rice harvested from the river's edge. The finishing touch was a one-by-one-inch removable framework that supported a canvas top to provide shelter from both sun and rain when needed. It was not a Boston Whaler or a Chris-Craft classic, but it actually promised to be a workable asset, if it didn't turn over and sink the first time it was set afloat. Now it was time to see if all this work would be an example of Peace Corps craziness, or cleverness.

The next morning about eight young workers from the village showed up all excited about the task assigned them: get Mr. Charley's boat in the water. There was just one problem. The door to the mud hut in which the boat was built was too narrow for the boat to fit through, no matter how it was angled or shoved. That's when one of the advantages of working in a mud hut became apparent; the guys simply hammered out a section to make the door wider and off we went, bound for the water. Besides the strong men that morning, almost everyone in the entire village gathered for the occasion. Everyone wanted to see what had been hidden in the hut throughout the height of the rains. A rope was tied to the bow cleat and then to a stake that was well-secured on the shore, and the boat-moving team gently lowered the craft into the river. The location that had been chosen was a quiet eddy so the current was not a concern.

Now afloat, the boat was bow-heavy, given all the reinforcements. But when Charles carefully installed the outboard motor to the transom, the weight of the motor trimmed up the vessel and it looked almost seaworthy. When he pulled on the starter cable, the engine roared to life and settled into a smooth throbbing idle. Charles called to the carpenter and invited him to join in the maiden trial, sitting on the starboard side.

With Charles pulling the shift lever forward and giving just the slightest throttle, the boat pulled from shore and they exited the calm water with trepidation. Immediately the boat felt right; it was responsive. It handled a little more throttle nicely and cut through the current it had now reached. Turning upstream, Charles rounded a bend in the river that placed them out of sight of Moira and all the spectators. He maneuvered the boat in every direction, testing its seaworthiness, making circles, hard turns, back and forth until convinced that the craft would not break apart from a poor design and workmanship or be unable to handle the force of the powerful current.

It worked well, steady as she goes. Then Charles cranked the throttle beyond the midpoint. He cranked some more until he reached full throttle and, to his delight, as one of the great points in his life, the boat's bow rose out of the water until the craft righted itself with only about three feet of the hull at the stern riding on the Little Scarsies. The boat was planing across the river surface, creating a wake that a 17-year-old on a jet ski would have found thrilling.

Just at that point, they rounded the bend and came in full view of the couple of hundred people waiting to see if the boat had sunk yet. A cheer rose up from the crowd, clapping and dancing, and the boat was unanimously named "Mr. Charley's Fly Boat" from that point forward. This was the start of a whole new world of work and wonder, as Charles would now be able to reach inaccessible village communities downriver. Large rock formations created whitewater rapids just upriver from Mange-Bureh, making that direction impossible. But the Little Scarsies flowed for 60 miles westward until it met the Atlantic Ocean at the delta, a huge confluence with the Great Scarsies River.

## Technology Transfer

One of the roles that a Peace Corps volunteer can fill is a bridge between village people and their interests and needs on one hand, and on the other, the various formal agencies whose staff members often prefer to remain in the capital cities and, with an elitist attitude, tend to keep a distance from village culture. Just a few years beyond independence, Sierra Leone still had a number of former colonial types working in-country. These "expats" continued to enjoy the beneficial lifestyle available to foreigners working in a developing country. It was apparent that some of them were unlikely to find work back in their own countries. Perhaps motivated by the best of intentions, after years of work, expats often slipped into a sense of entitlement, with a lifestyle that would be unattainable in their home economy. Cooks, nannies, gardeners, served in settings that were often approaching palatial. Inevitably, they looked down at the subsistence village and urban population. Charles found researchers at a British-funded rice research station were committed agronomists. He was impressed with their considerable knowledge of best practices in growing rice but frustrated at how unwilling these scientists were to assist in applying their findings at the village level, where it would provide major improvements to subsistence farming production levels. Here was an ideal role for a PCV as middleman.

During several visits to the rice research station, the agronomists provided samples of improved seed varieties and instructed Charles in techniques to disseminate seedlings and fertilizer. Having grown only a few vegetables with his dad in a suburban backyard, this was all foreign territory now. But he had a sense that this was the way to make a difference. With the boat providing a means to travel to so many rice paddies, and with Charles armed with improved seed varieties, a new program was forming. Combining this strategy with the hygiene and medical activities was making for a demanding daily regime.

The final months passed too quickly, and sooner than we wanted, our time in Sierra Leone came to an end. The months in Mange-Bureh had built for us a solid marital foundation, one that would help us weather future stresses common to most marriages. We still call that time our extended honeymoon. We went back five years later, but that is another story.

# 16.
## Kargbo

*Randy Cummings*

Kevin Farrell and I are Peace Corps Volunteers. We are "community development/rural development workers," and our job is to help the local people carry out projects they themselves identify and need. Villagers contribute their labor and the local government puts aside development funds for cement, rebar, and fuel. We act as catalysts and expediters. We also like to get in there and get our hands dirty, working right along with the people. We help build things such as bush roads, small bridges and culverts, wells for drinking water, and schools.

Kevin and I are stationed in Kabala, which is the capital of Koinadugu District, but we each live and work out in the chiefdoms. I live in a thatched-roof mud hut in Mongo Bendugu, a village of about 1200 people, the capital of Mongo Chiefdom. It is about a three hour drive by dirt road north of Kabala, around the other side of Mount Bintumani, the highest peak in the country. Kevin lives in similar circumstances in a chiefdom southeast of Kabala. Once or twice a month we drive our pickup trucks back to Kabala for gas and supplies. If we happen to meet up, we'll have a couple of beers and exchange stories about our life and work in the villages. We might complain a lot to each other, but we both really love doing what we do.

Kevin and I have been working mainly on prefabricated schools, a gift of the United States Agency for International Development (USAID). Back in the late 1950s, USAID gave a number of these schools to the district, but they sat in a warehouse and it wasn't until the Peace Corps arrived a couple of years ago that these schools began to get built. Many villages in Koinadugu's remote chiefdoms are without schools, and kids either have to travel a long distance to attend school or they don't go at all. A typical two-classroom USAID school can accommodate roughly 60 students per session, and schools often run two or three sessions a day. Working on a school is very rewarding. It's something I can point to with pride and say, "I helped build that."

A USAID school is simple in design. It's basically a steel framework that looks like something constructed out of a kid's Erector Set. The steel is surrounded by brick walls, with cutouts for wooden doors and window shutters, and it's finished off with a pitched roof of corrugated metal. Bricks are adobe-style, made by mixing a little cement with the area's red laterite soil, and then compressing it manually in a pressing machine. Dried in the tropical sun for three weeks, the bricks become rock-solid and are ideal for small-scale construction. Bricks are used for both the schools' outer walls and the interior walls that divide the classrooms. Flooring is mostly bare earth, unless funds are available for concrete.

Each classroom is 40 by 60 feet, so with its muted-red walls, brightly painted green doors and shutters, and shiny metal roof, a finished USAID school is indeed an imposing structure in a rural community. It's invariably the most substantial building around, and villagers take great pride in it, not least because they themselves helped construct it.

Although Kevin and I have been building schools for over a year, neither of us has ever built one from start to finish. When we arrived in-country several schools were in various stages of construction, and as money and labor became available we would work on that particular school. It is only now, three months into the second year of my tour, that I've had a chance to start a school from the beginning, here in Mongo Chiefdom.

My work counterpart is a Kuranko tribesman named Mohamaday Kargbo. He is the Koinadugu District Public Works Department Overseer for all the roads in the two chiefdoms where I work. Kargbo is a tall, slender, fair-skinned man, about 35 years old, with a narrow head, slightly protruding jaw, and prominent white teeth. He has wide expressive eyes and always looks like he's about to smile. Women find him attractive.

Kargbo is a man of significance in the chiefdom. Well-educated and holding an important government job, he is also descended from a branch of the Mongo royal lineage and is a dignitary in tribal matters. Commensurate with his social standing, he dresses stylishly in an African *dashiki* shirt and, depending on the season, either western long pants or roomy khaki shorts. He wears a colorful knitted *kufi* hat on his closely cropped head and imported brown leather sandals on his feet. Probably the most competent overseer in the entire district, Kargbo is loved by the scores of men who work under him. His supervisor in Kabala, Mr. Mansaray, with whom I meet once a month, can't say enough about Kargbo's intelligence and resourcefulness and the good work he does.

If Kargbo has a fault, it's his fondness for palm wine, the fermented sap collected from the wild date palms that grow along the streams in these parts. I occasionally have dinner with Kargbo and his friends in his compound, and afterward the men usually share a large gourd or two of palm wine. It's a refreshing drink and the light buzz it produces is enjoyable, but a few glasses give me an immediate headache and a whopping hangover the next morning if I have more than a few. Kargbo and the others, however, can drink the gourds dry and suffer no ill effects in the morning, no matter how much they've consumed the night before.

Kargbo has three wives and five kids, and from what I can observe he is a good family man. He treats his wives equally and kindly, doesn't sleep around, and is a doting father, especially to his only son. Kargbo is a Muslim, though not a very devout one. He fasts during Ramadan and usually goes to mosque each evening before dinner, but he doesn't pray regularly during the day and he disregards the prohibition against alcohol. I've heard it said that after the former chief of Mongo died, Kargbo lost the election to become regent because he isn't a good Muslim–he drinks. Regardless, Kargbo is popular and everyone enjoys his company and cheerful manner.

Working with Kargbo is a delight. He seems to know everyone, and through him I have met many people at all levels of chiefdom society. He's a gifted public speaker and a natural community organizer. I love to watch him slowly gain the confidence of a suspicious village chief and his staff, explain the purpose of our visit, and then deftly guide the discussion about what types of projects will best benefit the village and what the people need to do to get a project moving. Without Kargbo, I could never get the villagers' commitment to work on my projects. Indeed, without Kargbo I couldn't accomplish much of anything in the chiefdom.

Kargbo treats me like his younger brother, and I have deep affection for him. I try to repay his kindness by picking up things for him when I am in Kabala, buying him meals or cigarettes when we are on the road working, or perhaps transporting his friends and relatives when I am working on another project. Last year, for the Eid celebration at the end of Ramadan, I bought several yards of fabric, which the local tailor made into beautiful new clothes for Kargbo's family. In public, I always make it a point to defer to him and to show my respect by addressing him as Mr. Kargbo.

One day Kevin and I are together in Kabala and he asks if it would be okay for him to come to my chiefdom for a few days and work with me to put up the school I'm starting. He's planning to build a school in his chiefdom soon and wants to see how the steel framework is assembled and erected. I give him the date when we'll begin putting up the steel and tell him he's very welcome to join us. I like Kevin a lot, and having him visit and work together with me for a few days will be fantastic.

Actually, I have never raised the steel framework for an entirely new school. My only experience has been in helping another Peace Corps Volunteer put up the steel for additional classrooms at an existing school.

Additions are relatively easy because the existing school's columns help support the first set of new columns that goes up. The remaining columns and framework are then attached sequentially to the previously raised columns. Everything is solid and well-braced all along the way. Putting up a separate new classroom, however, is more complicated because there is nothing to support the initial columns and trusses while attaching the next line of columns. A solution is to pile large rocks at the base of each column and use long bush poles to brace and support the top of the structure as each section is raised. This is how I plan to do it in Mongo, and with both Kargbo and Kevin to help, I'm confident things will go smoothly.

My main concern is the construction schedule for this new school. We need to have the roof on before the heavy rains begin sometime next month. Once the roof is on, we can continue working through the rains, making bricks, putting up walls, installing doors and shutters, and so forth, Without a roof, all work will cease until the beginning of the dry season in December, and I won't see this school completed before my tour ends and I go home.

A few days after I return to my chiefdom, Kargbo and I gather some workers and begin laying out the steel at the site. This will be a two-classroom school, and each unassembled classroom now consists of about a dozen packages of steel strapped to wooden skids that were transported from Kabala to the site by truck a few weeks ago. Corner columns, support columns, girders, trusses, and purlins are all on separate skids. Two large wooden boxes hold all the nuts and bolts and connecting plates for the classrooms. Lastly, there are several bundles of sheet metal for the roof. Unpacking everything and making sure we have all the correct pieces and parts takes most of the morning.

The concrete pads on which the columns will stand were poured earlier in the month, so after the containers are unpacked we distribute all the steel and hardware around the corresponding pads. Next, we assemble the trusses and loosely attach them with bolts to the columns using the connecting plates. It's easy work, and we joke and talk nonchalantly in the warm afternoon. Everyone is feeling good about putting up this school, and we are glad for the villagers who will now have their own school.

Kevin arrives the day before we plan to start putting up the steel, and after a bucket bath to remove the dust from the road, he is treated to a meal of piquant groundnut stew and rice at Kargbo's compound. Kevin speaks Krio like a native and has a great personality. He and Kargbo get along instantly. After dinner and a quick walking tour of the village, several men of Kargbo's road crew join us. We sit around talking and drinking palm wine. Kargbo makes me the focus of a few of his stories and places me in a favorable light in the eyes of our new guest.

Early next morning, Kargbo, Kevin, and I reach the site. About 35 or 40 village men, along with a dozen workers from Kargbo's road crew, are waiting to help us. The sun has just barely burned through the morning mist, but already the heat is intense and the air is humid. Kargbo thinks we might get a little rain today.

The roof trusses are already connected to the tops of the column pairs, so our first step is to raise these assembled pieces and set them on the concrete pads. Next we'll join all the column-truss pairs with steel girders and then use purlins all along the roof to tie together the trusses.

A critical factor in USAID school construction is that everything must be square and aligned. If not, the walls won't be straight and the roof won't fit properly. After the columns are encased securely in concrete, it's impossible to rectify any lack of squareness. I worked on the roof at another school where the framework wasn't square, and I couldn't get the corrugated metal sheets to line up correctly. The finished roof not only looked awful, even from the road, but it leaked badly when it rained.

By noon the steel shell of the two-classroom building is standing firmly on its leveling pads. The villagers had raised the heavy pairs of columns and trusses using ropes and makeshift pulleys and brute strength; and young boys had scampered up the structure to assemble the girders and purlins and insert the nuts and bolts. All the columns are braced with large rocks at the base and long bush poles at the top; additional poles are placed strategically against the ends of the building and at the corners as a safety precaution.

Throughout the morning, we have heard the encouraging cheers and seen the waving arms and smiles of passengers in the colorful lorries as their drivers slowed down on the nearby road to take in the scene. By the time the building is up, a crowd of nonworkers has gathered to observe our progress, and the atmosphere is quite festive. Everyone appears pleased about the work.

By removing the bracing around a column, as well as some of the supporting poles, it's possible to adjust the position of each column on its pad until it's the correct distance from each of the other columns and is itself plumb and level. Bolts and nuts are only hand-tightened at this point, so there is a little slack to facilitate these modifications. Adjustment is rather crude—a forceful shove or a strong kick can correct most minor misalignments. If necessary, a crowbar and sledgehammer can complete the job.

Given the interconnectedness of everything, adjusting the plumb and distance of one column affects the plumb and distance of a neighboring column, and then another. While making the final corrections, several of the columns are actually freestanding, though most of the long poles supporting the top of the structure remain in place.

Kevin, Kargbo, and I are doing all the measuring and adjusting. There is a lot of shouting of directions, calling out measurements, and banging of hammers on the steel columns as we move things around and make the final corrections. Several workers help rearrange the supports as we move the columns into square. The others join the growing crowd of visitors and are standing nearby, talking and laughing and watching us work.

Well, you can guess where this is going. I am kneeling down on one of the pads with a crowbar, trying to adjust the last column. A number of the other columns are without support, standing freely on their pads. Thinking back on it, I swear I heard a swooshing sound, but I can't be sure. The next thing I know, people are shouting and screaming and running everywhere, and the whole structure begins slowly to tumble over. I duck down and cover my head.

It doesn't collapse completely. Just one corner buckles, but that causes everything else to twist and bend. The corner column has broken loose completely and is lying on the ground. The other columns, held up by only a few bush poles and the connecting plates, are all leaning toward the fallen corner. Bolts holding some of the connecting plates have sheared off, and a few plates are held by only a single bolt or two. The roof framework is still together but pitched severely toward the buckled corner. Three or four columns have shifted completely off their pads.

Although the steel framework toppled all around me, I'm not injured; but I am in a state of shock over what has happened. I stare in disbelief at the wreckage. Kargbo and the workers are also stunned and are now looking at me as if everything is my fault, which in some ways it is because I moved the column that caused all this steel to fall.

Kargbo appears unusually distraught and insists we stop all work completely and send a message to Mr. Mansaray in Kabala for assistance. While I fully understand that this collapse is going to result in some delay in construction no matter how we proceed, the last thing I want is to have this embarrassing twisted pile of metal sitting here for weeks while we wait for assistance from Kabala. I want to take it apart immediately and, if we can, start putting it back together.

Kargbo strongly rebuffs my recommendation, worrying that the building might fall further and injure or kill someone. He says we should just leave it for now until he gets word from Mansaray, and everyone, including Kevin, agrees with him. I refuse to give up and continue pleading my case, directing most of my argument at Kargbo, because without his support the villagers won't work, and the project is dead. We go back and forth rather vehemently like this for several minutes in the hot sun, but he remains adamant that there is nothing we can do.

Finally, frustrated and angry, I explode, "Listen, Kargbo, God damn it. I'm in charge here, this is my school, and you're going to do what I say."

"You are not my boss," he shouts back, the veins on his forehead rising and his eyes bulging with anger. "You cannot tell me what to do. Who do you think you are, speaking to me like this?"

We are now in each other's face. Kargbo's so close he's spraying me with spittle. We are both shouting and waving our arms wildly. Kevin steps forward and puts a hand on my shoulder, trying to calm me down. I jerk free and yell at him to shut up and stay out of it. I can see the disgust on his face as he backs away.

Kargbo and I go on with our dispute, though with less intensity now, and no longer at close range. A light rain begins to fall as my anger subsides, replaced by a sinking feeling in my gut and a vague overall sadness. I want to cry. I still can't believe this is happening. Everything is falling apart. I have lost my project, my friend Kargbo, Kevin's respect, my own self-respect, everything.

Regaining my composure, I tell Kargbo I'm sorry I behaved the way I did and for what I said. Again I make a case for taking the structure apart now, but this time with more logic and less emotion. I try to lay out clearly the advantages in resuming the work versus the disadvantages in abandoning it. I beg desperately for him to see it my way. "We can do this," I implore. "Let's at least try. Please, I really need your help." To my surprise, he relents and says he'll reconsider the situation. I am so relieved, I want to hug him.

The three of us return to the site and survey the damage. The steel columns are sound, and so are most of the trusses, but the majority of the connecting plates are badly bent and some of the girders and purlins are twisted. Kargbo says that the situation is not as bad as he first thought. A villager suggests we can get the local blacksmith to help straighten out the bent pieces.

The workers have been milling about quietly as if witnessing a road tragedy. When Kargbo calls them together, I can sense they have little faith in me now and probably despise me for attacking Kargbo the way I did. Kargbo carefully explains our plan and exhorts them to help us. He repeats some of the same arguments I had just made to him. Some villagers shake their heads and wander away, but most agree to go back to work.

By the end of the day, we have dismantled the building, and the blacksmith has magically straightened out all the bent plates, girders, and purlins; he has even managed to find some old nuts and bolts to replace those that snapped off. That evening Kevin and I again have dinner with Kargbo and his crew, but there isn't the camaraderie and cheer that imbued the previous night. In fact, everyone is rather sullen and we break up early. When we return to my place later, Kevin is silent. This is the first time we have been alone since the incident and I expect him to excoriate me for blowing up at Kargbo, but he says he's tired and goes to bed.

The next day we start again from the beginning. This time it is much more difficult because fewer than half the workers are present. Worse, none of the villagers will climb up on the scaffolding and the rafters to tighten the bolts. They are afraid it will come crashing down again. Kevin and I have to do it all ourselves. Even Kargbo won't climb up there. Final adjustments for plumb and squareness are also much cruder than yesterday because everyone fears removing too much of the bracing around the columns. The workers remove the long bush poles warily.

Finally, as the light begins to fade, the building is set once again on its pads. All the bolts are tightened, and the whole thing is about as square as can be expected. The next morning, we start pouring concrete sleeves around the base of the columns to hold them permanently. Kevin sticks around for an hour or so, but he's worked on schools at this stage of construction before, so he's not seeing anything new. I can tell that he's still offended by the way I treated Kargbo and probably wants to get as far away from me as he can. I thank him for coming up and helping us; he gives me a cool goodbye as he departs.

Outwardly, the relationship between Kargbo and me is quickly back to normal. Once the building started going back up, he seemed to have put the whole incident out of mind. We are talking and laughing just like before, as if nothing happened. But I doubt that he can ever completely forget our dispute. We've worked together almost daily for more than a year and this was the only time we've argued about anything. Moreover, I hurt him with my angry words and caused him to lose face before his people. In Kargbo's tribal society, such behavior is inexcusable.

We eventually finish the school, and I return to America. Back home, I often tell this story about the school collapsing. Assuming a self-deprecating manner, I pretend that the point of the story is my inviting a fellow PCV to watch my "expert" demonstration of how to erect a building and then having the whole thing collapse before his eyes. I never mention Kargbo, but whenever I relate the story I can't help thinking of him and the pain and humiliation I caused.

I returned to Sierra Leone in 1971 on the last leg of an African journey taken after I finished my first tour with USAID in Vietnam. I made it a point to visit Mongo Chiefdom, met once again my old friend Kargbo, and stayed overnight in his compound. One of his wives fixed a delicious rice dinner with chicken cooked in palm oil. Kargbo invited some of his friends to join us, and we all sat around drinking palm wine, talking, and laughing into the night. It was like old times. He told me at least twice that it was a great honor for him that I came especially to Mongo just to visit him. Neither of us mentioned the quarrel we had at the school construction site. He was my good friend, and more than 40 years later I still regret what happened that day.

# 17.
## Bombali Babee

*Robert Galeria*

M y first posting was to the village of Samaia, the headquarters of Tambaka Chiefdom, in the Bombali District. Tambaka was a Susu tribal area on the banks of the Little Scarsies River. The Temne language I had studied during our Peace Corps training went over like a lead balloon there; the Susu disliked the Temne and spoke only Susu.

The official list of my accomplishments is as follows: two bridge repairs and a medical clinic completed in Samaia; a water supply repair and school started in Fintonia; a culvert installed near the Guinea border; new rice strains introduced in Samaia; a bush access road initiated near Samaia; an orange plantation plan introduced in Kamakwie; and a large vegetable garden near Kamakwie encouraged with fresh American seeds that actually improved the crops, which were sold to the Lebanese shopkeepers and American missionaries in town. I was the unofficial wholesale distributor of Hollywood cigarettes, Parrot quinine tonic, and "margarine butter" to my friend Foday Drebah, the former lorry driver who owned the only shop in Samaia. I was his best customer. Said supplies were purchased on trips to Makeni or Freetown. That's the official version.

I did four dumb things while I was in Bombali. I was forgiven for all of them, I think.

The Peace Corps's egregiously bad training resulted in my declaring that my big celebratory welcome dinner, prepared by the chief's wives in front of the whole village, was not "sweet." I insisted that it was "hot," not yet knowing that in Krio, sweet meant "good." It was an awkward start, but my hosts were forgiving and remained so for my whole tour. I always believed that while they were comfortable with the assessment that "White man, *e tranga*" (strong) and "White man, *e get de sense*," they always felt a little sorry for us because we were not as handsome and beautiful as they were, and we were not Muslim. Proud Africans!

My second dumb thing was my crazed and threatening behavior during their semi-annual witch trials. When I investigated a large and noisy gathering and found a young woman chained to a log being berated and hit with switches, babbling and hysterical, I intervened physically in a big way. It didn't help when I was told that she was an admitted witch and that she was being forced to inform on others. They ignored me, and this went on for three days, just like in Arthur Miller's play, *The Crucible*. When it ended in the town chief's court with fines of five or ten Leones and a week or two of domestic service to be performed in the big men's homes in town, it was finally clear to me that this was just a regular soap opera-type entertainment, infrequently imposed on the out-of-favor households outside the village, which was immediately forgotten and not begrudged by anyone, including the victims.

My third dumb mistake was losing a leopard pelt the chief gave me to trade in Freetown for corrugated tin for a roof on his house. I stupidly entrusted it to the guard at the Peace Corps hostel, who upon my return had no memory of the transaction. This skin was valued at 39 pounds, and we were paid only 50 pounds a month, so I was in deep water on that. Fortunately the Peace Corps Director, George Peach Taylor, drew out money from petty cash when he heard about it, but my chief learned about it from spies and never thereafter entrusted me to transport the occasional elephant tusk he needed to sell in Makeni.

Finally, it's very hot in Samaia during the dry season, and the Little Scarsies River is shallow enough to wade across in many places. So of course I went for a swim in some of the larger, deeper pools. I was interrupted by a gang of "small boys" who screamed at me to get out of the river. When I did, they explained that big crocodiles, "de big fellah," were in those pools. They didn't let me go down to the river unescorted for weeks after that.

I was awakened by hysterical people after midnight one night during the rainy season, when the river runs in flood. One of the women of Samaia, accompanied by her husband, had just crossed the river in their dugout, and she had stayed behind to wash up. Her splashing in the water attracted a crocodile, which tailed her into the water and raked her back and arms with its claws and teeth and bit chunks out of her back. Fortunately the Wesleyan hospital was only about 26 miles away, in Kamakwie, but we had to roust the ferrymen out of bed to get my truck, "Bombali Babee," across the river, and they were reluctant. I went ballistic and threatened to get them all fired if they didn't cross us immediately. So we went across, the woman and three others in the back of my pickup, and the town chief and me in front. The missionaries were very good about the whole thing once we got there, and it was just like what you see on TV. I saw the woman again in Samaia about three weeks later, and she had some very scary-looking scars.

Two project failures stand out in my memory. The first was my attempt to bust a new road through the bush, to open up a few native grasslands, *bollis*, to dry land rice farming, using the cable winch on my truck to uproot small trees and bushes. It worked like crazy, completing the few miles in only two days, rather than the half a year it would have taken to do by hand. The only problem was that rather than creating a new road, our effort resulted in a narrow miles-long rice field that was appropriated by the local big men.

My second, and bigger, error was insisting on building the clinic for the people of Samaia on the banks overlooking the Little Scarsies River, rather than in the middle of the village, where they wanted it. I stupidly reasoned that a combination of the beautiful view (if you can believe that) and the cooling breezes coming off the river made the location on the cliffs mandatory. The clinic was built and finished to Sierra Leone government standards. It was the biggest structure in town and a serious bragging right over the surrounding territory. I really busted my chops on that project and was extremely proud of it myself. However, about a week after completing the building, on the first stormy day we had, the wind came up strongly off the cliffs along the river and peeled off the roof like the lid on a sardine can. We later re-roofed the building and made some structural modifications, locking down the four corners to solid pillars that ruined the aesthetics, in my opinion, but we got it done. I later learned that the Sierra Leone government failed to staff the place and instead used it somewhat as a school, though it wasn't really needed since the Catholic fathers had already established an elementary school in town.

I signed on for a third year with the Peace Corps, to be posted to Makeni, capital of the Northern Province. In Makeni I lived the high life, with indoor plumbing and daily electricity until 10:00 p.m. I was assigned to the teacher's college, under Father Rolli, where we used a CINVA ram machine, much admired by the Peace Corps for making compressed dirt bricks, and constructed a large assembly building with actual lumber and roofing, using paid labor. During this period I split my free time between Saffi's bar and pursuing VSO volunteer Jennifer Vaillant at the Banana Street teachers' residence.

I'm told the assembly building survived "the troubles" that decimated most of the large buildings in town as well as many of the small villages I frequented in my first two years. Upon reflection, I'd say there is good reason for Peace Corps not allowing everyone a third year. It was not as satisfying as my original assignment, although it certainly was on a personal level.

# 18.

## I Know Someone in Africa

*Gerry Cashion*

JFK's establishment of the Peace Corps fired my imagination. I saw the chance for adventure, free travel, and the opportunity to maybe do some good. When the legislation passed and Sargent Shriver created the agency, I immediately searched out an application. Though I would not finish undergraduate school until three years later, I guarded that application and finally submitted it to Washington 12 months before my anticipated graduation date. I had no idea whether my major and minor concentrations in English literature and political science would make my candidacy attractive to the Peace Corps, but I had done a lot of construction work to finance my university education and hoped that experience might give me some credibility.

Late in 1964, a Peace Corps letter arrived. I had been accepted and would be posted to Sierra Leone. I was thrilled; Africa is what I wanted. I had concluded that Americans generally did not travel to Africa unless they were well-heeled and going on a safari to East Africa or maybe to Egypt, to see the pyramids. Hell, most Americans didn't even know that Africa is a continent and not a country. Getting to Europe and South America was easy for Americans, even of limited means. But other faraway places, like the Dark Continent, were not likely.

So Africa it was, and I was ecstatic. When I informed my elder brother and his wife that I was going to Africa, wife Maryann said excitedly, "Hey, I know somebody in Africa!" I laughed. "You know somebody in Africa?" I thought to myself that among the 400 million people in Africa, my sister-in-law knows somebody. Well, she had worked for a while with Tom Dooley's MEDICO Foundation in Algeria. So it was both plausible and likely that she should know someone on the continent. "Yes, I worked in Algiers with a guy named John Van Damme, and I think he is still in Africa somewhere. Maybe you'll run into him." Now I thought this was absolutely comical but I humored her and said, "Well, you never know."

## Freetown and Fourah Bay College

Freetown, the capital city, was an old settlement created by the British as a refuge for freed slaves who supported Britain during the American Revolution and were rewarded with the option of being returned to Africa. Located on Fourah Bay below the Lion Mountain – Sierra Leone – for which the area had been named by the Portuguese, the city was characterized by charming, if somewhat dilapidated, colonial clapboard houses, impressive government buildings, a merchant class dominated by overseas Lebanese, and a hodgepodge of ethnic groups. The most influential were the Krios, descendants of slaves who had returned from North America and the Caribbean. They dominated the politics of colonial Sierra Leone right up until independence. The major indigenous groups – the Mende from the south and the Temne from the north – were well represented. People from other ethnic groups – the Limba, the Kono, the Mandingo, the Kuranko, and the Yalunka – inhabited pockets of the town, much like ethnic enclaves in major American cities.

We were treated to three days of orientation at Fourah Bay College before we departed to our designated postings. It is the oldest tertiary educational institution in West Africa. Founded in 1827, the college trained all the native civil servants who helped administer the British colonies of the Gambia, Sierra Leone, the Gold Coast (which would at independence become Ghana), and Nigeria. It was built high above the city like the colonists offices and dwellings in elevated locations – hill stations — that presumably were cooler and healthier, less vulnerable to diseases like Blackwater Fever that would generate Sierra Leone's reputation as the "White Man's Grave."

We began to explore Freetown. Kadra's Lebanese restaurant downtown was a discovery that got lots of patronage–great Middle Eastern food plus pretty good burgers. The KitKat Lounge was a watering hole. History beckoned us to the old City Hotel, where Graham Greene was reputed to have written *The Heart of the Matter*. Bob Golding, the CARE country director and head of our Peace Corps program, hosted a wonderful welcome get-acquainted party at his Lumley beachfront residence. That event allowed us to socialize among our group and encounter other volunteers who had arrived before us and had become country experts able to educate us newcomers. Much as we liked Freetown and the orientation, we were champing at the bit to get to our postings. So on our fourth day in Sierra Leone, we set off for our new posts.

## On to Kambia

I was posted to Kambia town, the capital of Kambia District, one of five districts that constituted the Northern Province. Six others in our Peace Corps group were also headed for Kambia. Experienced rural development volunteers Larry and Greg, who lived in Kambia town and were nearing the end of their service, were our drivers and guides. They knew "the ropes" and would help us settle in.

Upcountry, as the hinterland was known, was still relatively undeveloped in 1966. Apart from Lunsar, in the Port Loko District where the iron ore mines were situated, the Northern Province was pretty poor. As we would learn during our sojourn, northerners felt disadvantaged by the Sierra Leone Peoples' Party, the SLPP. It was dominated by the Mende, from the south, who were able to assume the reins of power at independence in 1961. Apart from the Fula ethnic group, northerners were generally supporters of the All Peoples' Congress, the APC. As elsewhere in Africa, ethnic politics prevailed in Sierra Leone, and the APC was the reviled opposition.

From Freetown, the trip to Kambia was a fairly easy day's drive if you didn't encounter long delays at the ferry crossing the Little Scarcies River or get bogged down in the mud of unpaved roads. A lunch stop in Port Loko introduced us to a favorite dish, Jollof rice, which was filled with the hot red pepper that gave birth to the name, the Marguerita, or Pepper, Coast. We were breathing fire and the old-timers Larry and Greg were thoroughly entertained by our misery.

Leaving Port Loko, we began to drive through 12-foot high elephant grass that lined both sides of the dirt road. Before long, our skin and clothing took on the red tinge of the lateritic dust raised by our vehicles. Crossing the Little Scarcies River required a ride on a barge-like welded-steel ferry that could accommodate two vehicles at a time. The Brits had located the crossing at a narrow part of the river. Our wait was short. Then we were on the ferry, and the crossing took about ten minutes. We continued north and the elephant grass enveloped us. How did Larry and Greg know where they were going? There were no road signs, no landmarks that we could detect, just tall grass. What did they see that determined where they would turn? We were mystified.

Many miles on, two of our group, Jack Ashburn and Mike Leckie, left our route and turned off west to head for Rokupr. They were posted to the rice research station there. Twelve miles farther north, the rest of our contingent entered Kambia town. Here Tom and Inger Crum split from us to continue west to their posting in Samu Chiefdom. They had to cross the Great Scarcies River by ferry to get there. David and Jude Barker continued some 40 miles north to the village of Kukuna, which was near the Guinea border in Susu country.

The Crums and the Barkers were to promote "chiefdom development" and were to lodge in the main village of their chiefdoms and work wherever opportunity was identified. I was designated as a "rural development" volunteer and was one of 12 of our group who were lucky enough to be assigned four-wheel-drive vehicles. We were located mostly in district capitals and expected to work anywhere in the district. Our task was to help civil authorities develop rural infrastructure: small bridges and culverts for rural roads, schools and health clinics. We would report to the district officer and engage closely with the Public Works Division.

Larry and Greg deposited me at the structure I would share with Ron, a volunteer primary school teacher who had arrived four months earlier, at the start of the school year. Our two-bedroom apartment was on the second floor of a concrete-and-block building located on the east bank of the Great Scarcies. A couple of general merchandise shops occupied the ground floor. The place was pretty basic. Besides the two bedrooms, it had a room with toilet, shower, and sink. It had a sitting room and a rudimentary kitchen with a sink, small refrigerator, and two-burner kerosene cooker. It sometimes had electricity and running water. Bare light bulbs hung from the ceiling. Not one's idea of luxury by any means, but very basic living quarters. The second floor elevation made it somewhat secure from thieves. I was satisfied.

Besides primary school teacher Ron, three female secondary school teachers also lived in Kambia town. As is the custom among Peace Corps volunteers, they had invited Ron, Larry, Greg, and me to dinner at their house that night. At sundown we gathered at their place, a three-bedroom concrete block house with sporadic electricity and water and a fairly fancy outhouse that they had nicely decorated. There was one other guest there that night and I was surprised to meet someone in Africa. He introduced himself as John Van Damme, who worked with CARE in Sierra Leone. It was a fine first evening for me in Kambia town.

Kambia town was a pleasant place with a few thousand inhabitants. It was a transit point between Conakry and Freetown. Its main drag was lined with Indian and Lebanese merchants. The local Chellarem's and the Choitram's were tiny versions of a fully integrated dry goods store. The essentials, such as canned food, cooking oil, toilet paper, beer, and soft drinks were available. Socialist Guinea had few consumer goods, so the shops served Guineans engaged in black market commerce, who smuggled purchases across the border. There were a couple of gas stations where fuel was supplied. A daily market offered a very meager selection of local vegetables, beef, lamb, and fish. An administrative park contained government offices and dwellings and tennis courts. A soccer field was a popular meeting place and matches drew lively crowds.

Because of its support for the opposition All People's Congress, Kambia District was not bestowed with lots of development funds. As a result, I had little construction work. I spent most of my time inspecting work already completed and writing reports on maintenance needs. I also helped draw plans for simple road works like culverts. From Rokupr, Mike and Jack assumed the role of agricultural extension agents and were busy delivering a new rice seed variety, Radin China 4, to local farmers for field testing. This lowland variety had been developed at the research station and yields on controlled test plots provided a substantially greater amount of swamp rice than what farmers were currently planting. Since I was under-employed, I also helped disseminate the new rice variety. Mike Leckie's baby chimpanzee Nelson accompanied him on excursions.

Life in Kambia was slow but pleasant. It was good to have other PCVs nearby, but I made friends with local people and became a great fan of the district soccer team. Occasional visits from CARE and Peace Corps staffers noted that I was not fully occupied. I was asked if I would be willing to transfer to another post. So it came as no surprise when I was asked to move.

## From Kambia to Bombali

Howard Gangestad had been posted to Makeni to serve as the RD volunteer for Bombali District. Howard was a 5'6" human dynamo who had been a wrestler at Mankato State University in Mankato, Minnesota. All muscle and no fat, he was always smiling, always happy. But one of his many sayings stuck with me: "If you're not having fun doing what you're doing, you shouldn't be doing it." According to legend,

Howard was one day driving back to Makeni from the northern part of Bombali District. At a point where the road was only wide enough to accommodate one vehicle, he encountered a large lorry full of timber that had broken down and was blocking the road. As the story goes, Howard enlisted a gaggle of local folks who had gathered near the lorry to help him unload the timber and stack it in such a manner as to build a ramp right over the truck. He intended to drive over the lorry, which he allegedly did. Once on the other side, he helped unstack the timber, reload it on the lorry, and then continued on his way to Makeni. Did we believe this yarn? Well, nobody we knew was an eyewitness, but none of us would say that this was beyond Howard's capability. He was that special kind of a guy.

Some six or seven months into his Makeni assignment, Howard decided that he wasn't having fun, so he left the Peace Corps and returned to Minnesota. This made the Makeni post vacant. CARE director Bob Golding considered the Makeni post more important than Kambia and asked me to move to Makeni. I made the move in August 1966, and this turned out to be an important turning point in my life.

Makeni was an inviting town and I settled in easily. It was the capital of the Northern Province and Bombali District. Makeni had 12,000 residents, much more commerce, and lots to do. Several PCVs and British volunteers, mainly teachers, worked in Makeni. The old narrow gauge railroad, a relic of colonialism and destined to disappear, terminated there. A road trip to Freetown could be done in half the time it took to go by train.

I was happy to have moved from Kambia. My residence was huge. It had regular running water and electricity. Its location near the center of town was convenient for transportation and shopping. The house had six bedrooms and was intended to be a refuge for volunteers posted outside of Makeni. They could come into town for the weekend or holidays and lodge at my place. PCVs who were traveling to or from their posts in other districts could pass the night. When Al Alemian was assigned to the Northern Province as an Assistant Peace Corps Director, he stayed with me for several weeks before he was able to move into his own place. Bob Galeria often came into town from his chiefdom in far north Bombali District. So my house in Makeni was a pretty lively joint.

One of the local officials I met soon after my move was Alimamy Dura, the leader of Tonka Limba chiefdom and the Paramount Chief Member of Parliament for Bombali District. He resided just a few miles outside Makeni in the principal chiefdom town of Binkolo. A small wiry

Limba man some 40 years old, Chief Dura had been educated in the United Kingdom. He was a hugely intelligent individual with an excellent command of English and an engaging smile. We became fast friends, and I learned much from him.

## The paramount chief educates the volunteer

One early benefit I derived from our relationship was Chief Dura's advice about my diet. As a bachelor who employed a houseman with no culinary artistry, my food regimen was fairly pathetic – unless, of course, I got an invite to dine with some of the female PCVs in town. My standard fare was white rice or spaghetti noodles with a palm oil meat sauce loaded with red pepper. I was regularly beset with stomach trouble. One day I was telling Chief Dura about my problem and he asked about my diet. When I told him about my usual fare, he said, "It's the oil and red pepper. They irritate your gall bladder. Stay away from them and your problem will disappear." This struck a chord because I remembered that my mother had to have her gall bladder removed. So I changed my eating habits, and indeed, my stomach problems ended.

Most PCVs brought some sort of skills to our assignments but few, if any, of us had any real knowledge about how to foster economic development. Here again Chief Dura was an educator. The road from Makeni to the northeastern district of Koinadugu passed through Binkolo. It was a lateritic dirt road. The only asphalt section outside of the district capital towns passed through the chief's town of Binkolo. It was about two kilometers long. Despite being a presumed supporter of the SLPP, the chief had secured funds for the asphalt paving from the central government.

Binkolo had no electricity, no piped water supply, no hospital, no industry, no bridges or culverts enabling year-round vehicle transport to the interior of the chiefdom, and few shops. In short, Tonka-Limba was undeveloped. It was curious to me, then, that the chief would devote precious funds to a stretch of asphalt over such other items you might think would be more important. When I asked him about this, the chief explained that this was the main road to the north. The dust raised by many passing vehicles smothered the entire town. People breathed dust 24/7. It was unhealthy. So devoting the development funds to a couple of kilometers of asphalt road through the town was a no-brainer. The asphalt substantially improved the quality of life in Binkolo.

The chief also educated me about the flora and fauna in the area. I had access to a small amount of funding to put in some culverts over seasonal streams in the district. Tonka-Limba Chiefdom was a priority target because of Alimamy Dura's influence. We could install some concrete culverts and also cut some trees and stretch logs over streambeds. However, I didn't know that we would spend so much time searching for the right trees to cut. As we walked through the bush to identify candidate trees, he would say, "No, that one is a great source of palm wine. No, this one is a sacred tree, we can't cut this one. Not any of these either. They belong to the Conteh clan." Like most people brought up in a rural setting, the chief intimately knew the value and use of Tonka-Limba's natural resources as well as who had use rights.

One of my adventures with the chief transpired when he took me to the Prime Minister's birthday party at the PM's residence at Lumley Beach. I was truly privileged to hobnob with some of Sierra Leone's big shots. The chief described their roles and political influence for me. Sir Albert, the Prime Minister, mingled with the crowd. It seemed there were also many ordinary people like me there, and I was impressed with the Prime Minister's outreach to the populace. One large room had a dozen huge serving tables laden with flowers on white linen tablecloths. Waiters were in the process of loading them with food for the many guests. Star beer and soft drinks were flowing. It was a convivial atmosphere on a beautiful day.

When the signal came that the crowd could approach the tables and serve ourselves, the guests rushed to grab a plate and fill it as fast as they could, apparently thinking that this gorgeous banquet would not last long. They were right. The crowd became a swarm of locusts. The tables were stripped clean in what seemed like seconds. What had moments before been plentiful offerings disappeared in the wink of an eye. It looked like a tornado had blown through the room. Empty bowls and platters littered the no-longer-lovely tables. Security personnel began to push people out of the room. I looked at the chief. He was angry. We left. I have never forgotten that scene.

## Marrying in Makeni

It was at Bob Golding's welcome party for our group that I first encountered the wonderful woman who would become my wife. Barbara Warren was part of the group of teachers that had arrived in August. I knew she was especially intelligent when she appeared disdainful of certain members of our group, led by Hugh McAllorum with his ever-present guitar, who performed a boisterous rendition of the Stones "We gotta get out of this place." Our singing was not politically correct.

Barbara taught science at the St. Joseph Girls' Secondary School which was run by Irish nuns. I got to know her little by little and was continually impressed by her dedication to her students. She devoted a lot of her spare time to students. It wasn't long before her dedication and charm had me roped into collecting specimens for her science classes. Things that could be dissected, such as lizards, geckos, and frogs, were especially important. Volunteers are excellent at improvising, part of the American genius, and Barbara was a great example. I soon fell into a routine whenever she beckoned. She would have a broom, and I would follow along with a container of some sort. When she found a spot populated by a sought-after specimen like the multicolored lizards with the bright orange heads, Barbara would smack them with her broom to stun and immobilize them and I would catch and deposit them in the container.

Barbara also devoted some after-school time to volunteer work at the Makeni hospital right across the street from my house. So if I were home, I would see her strolling to the hospital to work as an assistant to the medical officer in charge, Dr. Samuel Banda. In most third-world medical facilities, the staff is overworked and underpaid. Funding, equipment, medicines, and supplies are inadequate. As a result, people find creative ways to cope and become multi-talented, often performing procedures for which they have little or no training. So it didn't surprise me that Barbara was soon considered part of the staff and even helped Dr. Banda in his rudimentary surgical theater. I would often get together with Barbara after her work at the hospital, and she would tell me about her latest accomplishment.

One afternoon after her stint at the hospital, we sat enjoying a Star beer at Safi Daramy's bar just a hundred yards down the street. Barbara told me that she had just drained a hydrocele. "Drained a what?" I asked. "A hydrocele. This is a build-up of fluid in the testicles. This man came into the hospital with testicles the size of basketballs. I was surprised that he didn't come in carrying them in a wheelbarrow. Well, I had to make a small incision in each testicle and drain the fluid. Then I stitched him up." I sat there somewhat dumbfounded listening to her. Finally I asked, "Doctor Banda lets you do this kind of stuff?" "Oh yeah, as long as I wash and use the antiseptic and such." I was impressed. This woman is something special, I thought. "Well, I guess that's just what a PCV is likely to do in her spare time," I laughed. This

Barbara Warren was growing on me. As time went on I learned that she could drive a three-quarter-ton four-by-four pickup on the dirt roads as well as any man, enjoyed jazz (as did I), was smart as a whip, and a lot of fun, in addition to being mighty good-looking.

To make a long story short, Barbara and I decided to marry. I don't know if I proposed to her or she proposed to me or we both proposed to each other, but we were going to get married. We set the date for Saturday, April 1. Spreading our good news among our PCV pals and other friends, we were met with skepticism and even derisive guffaws. Sure. April 1. Right. Hardy har har. But we finally convinced people that it was not an April Fools' joke and that the choice of date was based on church availability, the Easter school break, and other such factors.

The planning was fun. And the contributions of friends were amazing. One of the tasks I almost forgot was to get permission from the Bishop of Makeni to get married in his Catholic church. "Cherry," the Bishop said to me, "you have never even seen the inside of my church and you want to get married in it?" The northern province of Sierra Leone was staffed by Catholic religious who were all Italians. "But Bishop, of course I have been to your church," I lied. "Cherry, if you want to get married in my church, you better be there for next Sunday's mass." "Yes, Bishop." It was a Palm Sunday, and I was there, so the Bishop gave us his blessing.

Meanwhile, my wife-to-be was raised a Southern Baptist but she graciously agreed to marry in a Catholic church. Neither of us was terribly religious and had not been attending any services, but we decided on the Catholic church because all the other churches in Makeni were holy roller kinds of institutions, the Italian priests were pretty cool characters and a lot of fun, and I was nominally a Catholic.

Barb and I had to decide whom to ask to accept various tasks. Who would marry us? Who might constitute the wedding party? Who would stand in for Barbara's father to give her away? Who would be the Maid or Matron of Honor? The Best Man? We made our decisions and then began to ask people if they would help us. The responses were amazing.

St. Augustine Teacher Training College was located right across the road from Barbara's girls' high school. Father Romano Rolli was principal of the college, and we often socialized with him and other of the Italian clergy. Father Rolli was a great guy so we asked him to perform the ceremony for us, and he agreed. Because the college would be on spring break the weekend of our marriage, he also offered the dormitories as lodging for relatives and friends who might come to Makeni to celebrate with us.

George Peach Taylor, the Peace Corps director, agreed to be the surrogate father. Harry Kightlinger, the deputy Peace Corps director, was to be Best Man. Diane Kightlinger, Harry's wife, the Matron of Honor. My groomsmen were Bob Galeria, Dick Palmateer, Roger Robison, Norman Davidson (a British volunteer), and Ira Manley, a Sierra Leone law enforcement officer who was a member of the Special Branch and had served as the Prime Minister's bodyguard. Barbara's attendants were teaching colleagues: Bonnie Bechtel and Helen Holt, two PCVs, and Jennifer Vaillant, a British volunteer who was destined to become Mrs. Bob Galeria.

Our pending marriage generated so much enthusiasm that we received an amazing number of contributions and help to pull it off. Tony Reed-Brooke, the Northern Province representative of the British American Tobacco Company, offered us the BATC guest house in Makeni as a wedding-night lodging. He also offered to host the reception on the BATC compound. Our pal Al Alemian, the assistant PC director, put up our VIPs at his house. All the PCV residences in Makeni welcomed out-of-towners. Ira Manley offered his car and chauffeur services on the wedding day. The Irish nuns at Barbara's school made a three-layer wedding cake loaded with rum. The Sierra Leone Brewery provided several cases of Star beer and boxes of glasses. The Sierra Leone Electricity Corporation strung lights at the BATC compound free of charge. The nearby school lent tables and chairs. Roger Robison created a stunning bride's bouquet made of frangipani blossoms. Barbara, an accomplished seamstress, so I learned, made an absolutely stunning wedding dress for herself. Several volunteers planned a menu and helped cook meals at the college for the many out-of-towners who honored us by coming from all parts of the country for the April 1 weekend.

So the April Fools' Day came, and we were married by Father Rolli. At least, we thought we were. Fr. Rolli had never done a wedding so he seemed to wing it, and several moments occurred when none of us knew what to do. But we got through it happily, and Barb and I retired to the BATC guesthouse, our wedding night cottage. Late in the afternoon, a fine wedding reception began on the compound. I had been able to access a major portion of my readjustment allowance to help finance the reception. With lots of food and drink contributions from the guests as well, everyone was well spirited and fed. Our many Sierra Leonean friends said that our wedding was the major Makeni social event of 1967.

Having devoted the funds from my readjustment allowance to feeding the out-of-towners and to the reception, Barbara and I didn't have a lot of money to spend on a honeymoon. So we decided to travel the short distance to Monrovia, Liberia, and stay a few days at the Ducor Palace hotel. At the time, this was one of the holdings of the Intercontinental Hotel chain owned by Pan American Airways and one of the best hotels in West Africa.

Unbeknownst to Barbara and me, our friends, who knew about our honeymoon plans, had taken up a collection to send us to a different destination. They presented us with a surprise at the reception: enough dough to go to Las Palmas, capital of Spain's Canary Islands, for our honeymoon. We were overwhelmed. But go to Las Palmas we did, where we stayed in a fully furnished apartment with maid service for $2.85 a day, a chateaubriand steak dinner could be had for 35 cents, and an empty wine bottle could be refilled from a cask for 17 cents.

## We go cut off their heads like chickens

Albert Margai had succeeded his brother, Milton Margai, as Sierra Leone's second Prime Minister. As the head of the Sierra Leone's Peoples' Party, Sir Albert played ethnicity to the hilt, favoring the southern Mende over the second most populous group, the Temne, who resided mainly in the northern half of the country. He also tried to eliminate party politics by creating a one-party state. So politics effectively pitted the south against the north. Other groups – the Krio of Freetown, the Limba and Kuranko of the north, the Kono of the east, the Mandingo, and the Fula were split in their political loyalties.

A general election was scheduled for March 1967, just before our wedding. Heated campaigning made us nervous, and we hoped that nothing would disrupt our marriage plans. The election went off mostly without incident, but when Siaka Stevens, the opposition party All Peoples Congress candidate won in a major upset, things quickly deteriorated. The Governor General had declared Stevens the official winner and set the date for his swearing-in. But General of the Army David Lansana intervened and placed Stevens and the Governor General under house arrest. Two days later another general, Juxton-Smith, overthrew Lansana, and senior officers created the National Reformation Council.

# A third year

Barbara and I had decided we would volunteer to remain for a third year of service. The Peace Corps director agreed and provided us with air tickets for a visit home before beginning the third year. When we returned to Makeni, we resided in our own little apartment. Barb had moved out of the house she shared with three other volunteers, and I had vacated the RD house. Our apartment was on a second floor above a shop across from the lorry park situated below Wusum Hill.

Barbara continued to teach at St. Joseph. I was still assigned to Makeni, but I had been recruited by John Roach, an Irish expatriate who served as agricultural officer for Koinadugu District, to help him build a major agricultural complex just outside the district capital of Kabala. To do this I had to spend much of the work week there. So I began to commute to Kabala for four days each week. With the clear vision of hindsight, I recognize that this was one of the first mistakes in my marriage. I had taken Barbara out of the comfortable house shared with her fellow teachers right near her school and relocated her to our apartment on the other side of town. Now she spent several evenings alone each week while I was in Kabala and the social fabric of life in Sierra Leone was deteriorating because of the political impasse. I liked my new job, but I should have rejected Roach's offer.

Police and members of the military had begun to harass students and presumed supporters of the SLPP. Fula tribesmen were a target. One Saturday, Barbara and I watched from our apartment as Temne and Limba thugs chased down Fula and beat them mercilessly in the lorry park. Another day, police went to St. Francis Secondary School and beat students. When the principal, a member of the Dutch Christian Brothers' Order that ran the school, went to the Makeni police headquarters to complain, he was dismissed by the colonel in charge and received a rifle butt to the face, which cost him an eye.

One evening in Kabala after work, I was drinking a beer with PCV friends at Lansana Kamara's bar and dry goods shop near the Kabala lorry park. An APC member of parliament with an electric bullhorn began to address a gathering crowd in the park. A.B. Kamara was well known to us because we were working in his district. We could hear what was being said. He started with a prolonged harangue denouncing the SLPP and its supporters. Then with a glance our way and speaking in Krio, surely for our benefit, he began to rail against the Peace Corps. "We will chase them in the street like dogs. We will cut off their heads like chickens." This was an ominous warning and L.K., as we called Lansana Kamara, suggested that we should depart. He feared the crowd could become dangerous. We were able to slip away unharmed but this incident made an impression.

Dissatisfaction with the National Reformation Council became widespread and in April 1968 another coup led to its demise. What became known as the "sergeants' coup" dissolved the council and led to another short period of chaos. There seemed to be no leadership.

One Friday afternoon, Al Alemian was driving back to Makeni and was stopped at a roadblock just outside of town. An armed group of drunken corporals and privates grabbed his truck keys and threw them off into the bush. Somehow Al was able to extricate himself from the soldiers, retrieve his keys, and continue to Makeni.

On a Saturday morning Barbara and I were shopping at Pa Keister's dry goods store on the main road in Makeni. There were several armed soldiers in the shop harassing Pa Keister and demanding gifts. I had parked my Chevrolet pickup in front of the store. When we completed our purchase, Barb and I got into the truck. Meantime, someone had parked a small motorcycle behind the truck. I didn't see it and when I backed up a bit to exit my parking space, I tapped the motorcycle. Seeing this, some of the soldiers ran from the shop, ordered us out of the truck at gunpoint, demanded my keys, and said we would be marched to police headquarters to be charged with property damage. There had been no damage whatsoever to the motorcycle, not a scratch. So we started walking down the road toward Makeni's main roundabout, prodded by sten gun barrels in our backs. After a couple of hundred yards, there was an argument between the soldiers, and we were ordered to turn around and march back to the truck. So we reversed and, again, after we had reached the truck another heated discussion took place. We were turned around and resumed our march to the police headquarters. By now a sizeable crowd had gathered to watch this spectacle. At some point, a corporal recognized Barbara and me from work I had done in his village. He intervened with his colleagues and after about five minutes of cajoling, he managed to get us released, gave me my truck keys, and told us to be on our way.

Another evening several of us were in a bar called the Wusum Club, where we often gathered to drink a beer and dance. About seven shirtless soldiers with rifles came in and began to demand beer from the owner. We sensed that this was a dangerous situation and started to discreetly slip out of the bar, one by one. All of us departed safely. When our third year of service ended, Barbara and I were not unhappy to leave Sierra Leone.

Colonel John Bangura assumed the military leadership soon after the sergeants' coup, released Siaka Stevens, and the All People's Congress took the reins of power. Stevens was succeeded by another ineffectual Limba man, Joseph Momo, and Sierra Leone continued its descent. Thugs like Lansana Bangura, Major Johnny Koroma, and ultimately Liberia's Charles Taylor fomented ethnic and civil strife and looted the country. Blood diamonds bought arms. Child soldiers maimed adults and adult soldiers maimed children. Many years passed before a U.N Peacekeeping force could halt the slide into hell.

## A phoenix?

In June and July of 2006, I traveled to Africa to evaluate the programs of the International Foundation for Education and Self-Help. This task would take me to several countries, including Guinea and Liberia in West Africa. Commercial air travel and connections in West Africa remain terribly difficult. Thus, completing our work in Guinea, my colleague and I decided to drive overland from Conakry to Freetown, where we could get a flight to Monrovia. An IFESH vehicle and driver would transport us. I was pleased to find a bridge spanning the Great Scarcies River where formerly a ferry crossing was required. I was eagerly anticipating my first visit to Kambia town since my departure 40 years earlier. I knew the town had been the site of much of Sierra Leone's troubles.

We drove into Kambia and saw that the town had been destroyed; little remained. The many commercial establishments on the main road were in ruins. Not one was standing. The town had been largely abandoned. To my surprise, my residence on the river bank was still there, seemingly untouched, its green paint faded into a nearly colorless tint. How and why did it survive? As we continued on to Freetown, it appeared that the countryside was barren of people. Where had everyone gone? Our arrival in Freetown supplied a partial answer. I didn't recognize the city I had known. The streets were jammed with people and vehicles and a cacophony greeted us. The countryside had emptied into the city.

The next morning, we went to a helicopter pad at Cape Sierra Leone where we were to board a big old Russian transport helicopter, one of two operated by Paradise Airways. The chopper would carry us and 22 other passengers on a 10-minute flight to Lungi airport. There we would get our plane to Monrovia. I thought about the name of the company. Paradise was an optimistic name, perhaps a good one. After all, Sierra Leone's future is looking brighter now that Charles Taylor and other thugs are out of the picture. The Kimberly Accord has limited the flow of blood diamonds. Sierra Leone's people are resilient.

Two weeks after I flew Paradise Airways, one of its helicopters crashed, killing everyone aboard.

# 19.
## Agent of Change?

*David Read Barker*

T he posting was so startling that it took hours for it to begin to sink in: Judith and I were not going to serve in a Temne-speaking chiefdom but were being sent to Susu territory. All that effort to learn Temne was flowing rapidly down the drain. How could they do this to us, who had been among the most diligent and successful Temne students? The simple answer, from Bob Golding, our boss at CARE, was, "Well, we figured since you were so good at learning Temne, you could easily pick up Susu."

So we were going to live in Kukuna, the main town of Bramaia Chiefdom, in the Kambia District. I wrote home, "As usual, the PC screwed things up because our chiefdom is in a Susu tribal area, and the Susu language is no closer to Temne than English is. All that hard work for nothing...."

We were the first PCVs to be posted in Bramaia Chiefdom, but we were not the first to work there. In 1964, two PCVs built bridges across two streams. Then in 1965, a PCV conducted a one-day "Chiefdom Survey" of Bramaia Chiefdom. He reported, "There were some problems generated at the district level by reports from a volunteer of forced labor, beatings, and poor cooperation and lack of interest on the two bridges done by the Peace Corps in this chiefdom." He concluded, "This chiefdom does not seem to be one of the more favorable ones for chiefdom development. There is the problem of the indifferent chief and of a group of people who are fairly satisfied with things as they are. There is also the fact that there is an established mission in town. The chiefdom, in addition, is quite isolated from the rest of the district and from the rest of the North."

Until the morning of our arrival, no one informed anyone in Bramaia that two PCVs would be coming to live in Kukuna. In mid-January 1966, the District Officer escorted us to Kukuna for a formal introduction to the chiefdom. His entourage included a projectionist who set up a generator-operated projector and screen in the main public square. The film was a Disney cartoon, introduced by the cute fairy whose magic wand sprinkles sparkly stardust. The crowd greeted the fairy with wild applause and the demand to show and re-show that few-second segment. I have no memory at all of what the cartoon story was, only the cheers for the fairy.

My journey to Kukuna began while walking back to my college dorm after music appreciation class. The radio was blaring from a convertible with its top down. "The President has been shot in Dallas." The date was 22 November 1963. John Kennedy inspired me to ask what I could do for my country. During the 21 months after his assassination, Judith (then known as Jude) and I met and married, I graduated from the University of Pennsylvania, and we began Peace Corps training. I was to be an Agent of Change, which as I understood it was thoroughly comingled with Progress, which brings Prosperity and Social Justice. These might not come until after we had completed our Peace Corps service, but surely they would arrive within a few years.

My qualifications to be an Agent of Change were painfully limited. I had participated in several nonviolent sit-ins and had picketed the Woolworth's department store in Philadelphia to protest the segregation of soda fountains in their southern stores. And I had written an undergraduate paper about how local environmentalists stopped the New York Port Authority from building a huge airport on the Great Swamp near Morristown, NJ. Unlike nearly everyone else in our group, I had already visited Africa. As an undergraduate international relations major, I had gotten a research grant for a three-week visit to Accra, Ghana, to study its role in the non-aligned movement, a whirlwind tour limited to the capital and its suburbs, conducted entirely in English. These experiences taught me to expect quick, decisive results. I thought that Sierra Leone would be pretty much like Philadelphia or New Jersey or Accra.

We never recovered from the blow of being stationed in a place where we couldn't even say "Hello" on the day we arrived. It was months before we understood what people in Kukuna were saying in their greetings. One adult greeting another would say, "*Tana mu Feye, Tana mu Feye,*" to which the other would reply, "*Inuwali, Inuwali.*" The direct translation of these terms are "There are no evil affairs" and "I am working." But the meaning was, "I am not practicing witchcraft on you" to which the reply was, "Yes, [I know that because] I am working."

The Peace Corps staff, and we ourselves, had very high expectations. It had been intimated to government officials in Freetown and Kambia that I had advanced technical skills in civil engineering, particularly water supply and road and bridge construction, and that I could accomplish complex projects in very little time. In fact, the totality of my relevant experience was one summer as a day laborer for a suburban paving contractor.

Initially, the D.O. told me to build a water supply for Kukuna, by tapping into the Great Scarcies River, three-fourths of a mile away, pumping the water by diesel to a cistern at the highest point in town, and feeding it by gravity to 20 faucets scattered around town. Timeframe: two months. It was a completely unrealistic project for which there was no construction money on hand or any way to raise any money and no means to pay for the diesel fuel and maintenance, even if the construction money were found. A couple of months later, the D.O. told me that I should build two bridges before the fiscal year ended.

Expectations in Kukuna were much murkier. A member of the Bramaia Chiefdom committee told me that the PCVs who preceded us generated a great deal of resentment during the construction of the two "Peace Corps" bridges, neither of which was a particularly neat job. One bridge had no side rails, and rebar stuck out all over the abutments and side rails of the other. Also, the PCV's report of forced labor was a "misinterpretation of the facts," according to my informant. All in all, the bridges were not satisfactory, and he told me that if my work was not better than theirs, my presence would no longer be desired.

When our neighbors in Kukuna asked why we had come to Sierra Leone, I would usually say, "John Kennedy sent me." That made sense to me, but our neighbors said, "Only a lunatic would want to leave the United States to live in Kukuna." We rarely thought that anyone might want to harm us; on the contrary, our neighbors kept a close eye on us, perhaps fearing unfortunate consequences for them if anything bad happened to us.

Before we arrived, there had been no collective discussion about how we could best be used, and subsequent months spent trying to figure this out produced only frustration all around. We never could align local expectations (vast or completely indifferent, depending on whom you asked), my technical skills (very modest, to put it politely) and the budget (nonexistent). Since the local Peace Corps and CARE staff and

149

Sierra Leone government officials were senior to us in age and rank, it was convenient for them to suggest that somehow we had brought our troubles onto ourselves, a view that we gradually internalized. Our monthly reports to CARE, which were expected to enumerate our tangible accomplishments in bringing about "change" and "development," only served to intensify my feelings of inadequacy. Simply surviving in Kukuna came to feel like an accomplishment in itself.

Kukuna, the main town of Bramaia Chiefdom, consisted of a dusty, rut-filled motor road lined on both sides by about 150 mud-block houses with thatch or corrugated steel roofs. There were about 2,000 people and about 20 tiny shops owned by local people. The appearance of the town had changed a great deal in the previous 10 years or so. In 1953, the British colonial government constructed the motor road from Kambia, 35 miles away. Traditional Susu houses were round and made of wattle and daub, with a conical thatch roof. The road made possible a new style of house: rectangular, constructed of mud blocks, with corrugated "tin pan" hip roofs.

Our house, like many others, was built of cement-plastered mud blocks with a galvanized corrugated hip roof, whitewashed inside and out. It had opening windows with wooden shutters and iron *tief* bars to keep unwanted people out. The floors were concrete. In one corner of the living room a large metal tank collected water from the roof by a simple gutter and plastic pipe. Our bedroom was in the front, to the left of the front door. Once we got used to it, the mosquito netting surrounding the bed helped make us feel protected. I built a shower in the back left room, set below the level of the floor, with a drain through the outside wall. Local carpenters made the wooden furniture. Our prized possession was a kerosene refrigerator that could make ice cubes. The Peace Corps gave us a book locker filled with paperbacks. One wall was decorated with the poorly-tanned skins of an 18'3" python.

In the evening, our house was usually full of kids; we had 40 or 60 "regulars" and up to a hundred for any sort of "special" event. The children behaved very well and followed our instructions, a small price for them to pay for the right to watch us intently. Sometimes we interacted with them, trading English and Susu vocabulary, but they seemed just as happy if we buried ourselves in a book and ignored them. Occasionally some women from next door would drop by in the evening, but the men almost never did. Like everyone else in town, we kept chickens around the house. The chief gave us a rooster and a hen the day we arrived, and we soon bought another hen, for 60 cents. The chief's rooster died of unknown causes, but we kept the hens in a grass pen in the backyard. They gave us very few eggs.

The changing seasons in Kukuna remain among my strongest memories. Although Sierra Leone dubbed itself the "Land of Iron and Diamonds," we thought it was a land of dust and mud. Sometimes the rain fell in such torrents that you feared you might drown just standing in it.

The road initiated the transition from a subsistence to a peasant economy in which the local groundnut crop could be traded for rice, and ginger could be sold for cash in Kambia or Port Loko. Population growth in Bramaia was increasing demand for food and consequently bringing more land under cultivation. In the local slash-and-burn agriculture, this meant reducing the time that formerly cultivated plots were left fallow. People said that the cycle has been reduced by half, to eight to twelve years, from 18 only a generation earlier. The chief controlled all of the "heavy bush," which had grown untouched for several decades or more. An order from the chief to cut the heavy bush meant a lot of physical labor and spiritual terror. The heaviest bush in Bramaia is real jungle, with trees a hundred feet high and six feet in diameter. It was terribly difficult work using only machetes, the heaviest cutting tool available. But this was minor compared with the problem that cutting down the largest trees freed their tree devils. I watched men confronting a huge tree, wailing, "Please, Devil, don't kill us. The Chief ordered us to cut down your tree."

Expanding cultivation reduced native habitat and increased direct conflicts between people and dominant animals: baboons, elephants, crocodiles, and snakes. The baboons lived in family groups of 15 up to 40 individuals. They were particularly attracted to ripe fields of groundnuts, which they dug up with glee. It was an awesome sight to watch a big baboon family, males out at the perimeter of the field, mothers and children in the center, foragers digging and poking here and there. The Susu said that if you shot one, they would run. If you shot two, they would stop, and if you shot three, they would attack and kill you. People generally respected the baboons and avoided them.

The flat seasonally flooded wetlands in the north of the chiefdom, near the Great Scarcies River, attracted elephants. Since the wetlands support many species of native grasses, the farmers found that they could get good yields of cultivated rice in these places. But the rice attracted elephants, which created even more havoc with the rice than the baboons did with the groundnuts. One of the last elephants in Bramaia was killed while we were there.

Women who frequently washed their clothes and got their household water from the Great Scarcies had a great fear of crocodiles, which snatched women and children often enough to require a high level of alertness. We bought the hide of a local seven-and-one-half-foot croc from some villagers, but it stank and we eventually threw it away.

Our neighbors hated all snakes with a passion and made every effort to kill every one they saw. The snakes—especially the mambas and the spitting cobras—almost scared me out of my wits. The mambas were famous for hanging out in the branches above footpaths and dropping on the back of your neck as you walked along; death would come in a few minutes. The spitting cobras hid in the grass and could blind you from six feet away. Lorry drivers were notorious for swerving wildly to run over a snake sunning itself on the road.

At first, the spiders were the creepiest critters of all. Touch your middle fingers and thumbs; that is the size of the spiders. Since they ate bugs and had no interest in us, we quickly got used to them.

Throughout my whole time in Kukuna, I was painfully aware that I could understand only a little bit of what was going on around me in the village. One evening several months after we arrived, I experienced the Spirit of the Drums, which entered the drummers who were providing an aural pathway through the drums between their spirit world and the ordinary world of the crowd. The drummers' entrancement flowed outward through the crowd, beyond the range of the pressurized kerosene petromax lamps, to the darkest outer reaches of Kukuna. I experienced the Spirit of the Drums as a malevolent force. It was hard not to connect the Spirit of the Drums to the Devils who were being driven off their trees as the heavy bush was felled. Somehow you knew that the Devils were likely to be right when they said that the people would have hell to pay for cutting the jungle.

Kukuna was described by its residents as being a completely and devoutly Muslim town, so much so that no beer was sold in town. I enjoyed visiting the two Koranic schools in town because it was so interesting to hear the young boys tackle their Arabic lessons, reciting the Koran at the tops of their lungs. I visited the mosque a few times but never stayed for worship.

The chief always served a collective meal at his compound for the men who had attended mid-day prayers on Fridays. Food was served in two or three large metal cauldrons filled with rice topped with chilies and a little tomato sauce with bits of meat. The men squatted around the cauldrons and reached in with their right hands to grab mouthfuls of food. The traditional Islamic punishment for chronic theft is cutting off the right hand. The right hand is clean and is used for eating; the left hand is dirty and used for the toilet. One man, with no right hand, ate entirely by himself. He was forever cut off from the communal bowl because of his thievery.

At about the same time that the road from Kambia was built, the American Wesleyan Methodist (AWM) mission opened a primary school in Kukuna. Almost from the beginning there was conflict with the AWM missionaries over their emphasis on teaching evangelical Methodism to the children of devout Muslims. The husband-and-wife American missionaries, the Nymans, had completed three years in Kukuna and were on home leave most of the time Judith and I were there. We overlapped with them for a couple of months. They lived in a big house just outside town, spoke almost no Susu, and loved to play Monopoly. The missionaries had not made a single Christian convert in Kukuna in 25 years. Although the school was an obvious possible place for us to establish ourselves in the town, we were very reluctant to work there because of the general negative attitude toward schooling, due partly to the late chief's personal dislike of the school, partly to the AWM missionaries' aggressive Christianity, and partly because Susu fathers believed, correctly, that their sons would not want to be farmers if they were educated.

Superficially, the Nymans and the Barkers had a lot in common. We were both idealistic, White American Agents of Change. But Judith and I saw nothing wrong with being a Muslim and had no interest in converting the Susu to Christianity. For their part, the Nymans had no apparent interest in promoting economic development. The motivations that had brought us to Kukuna were so different that we found it difficult to relate to one another.

Despite the chiefdom's lack of money and my lack of confidence in my skills, I completed a few small projects. A crew of men from Kukuna dug a shallow well at a low spot on the path to the river; the women loved being able to collect water closer to their homes, but the men were fearful that bodies of their "enemies" would be thrown into the well. Another crew built a concrete culvert to replace a small palm-log bridge to a village near Kukuna, enabling lorries to reach the village year-round. And I earnestly promoted improved laying hens despite the widespread skepticism that it made sense to feed them; without feed, they either died or gave no more eggs than normal Kukuna chickens, which survived with almost no care. But despite my best efforts, I could not satisfy the CARE bosses in Freetown and the District Officer in Kambia, all of whom seemed unhappy about my "accomplishments."

Life in Kukuna gradually became an ordeal that mixed stupefying boredom, terror of snakebite, sorrow at being unable to communicate with my neighbors, and the thrill of living such an adventure.

Then we began to hear of the re-emergence of the Leopard Society. What the Leopard Society actually was, and who its members were, were never clear at all, but they were said to be stealing babies at night, and eating them in the jungle. Our neighbors were terrified of the Leopard Society, and this rubbed off onto us. The resurgent Leopard Society, combined with Judith's unfortunate encounter with the new Paramount Chief, recounted in the next essay, created such an atmosphere of insecurity that we decided that we had to leave.

The staff at CARE tried to find us a new post for the remaining nine months of our tour of duty, but the thought of trying to learn a third tribal language in one Peace Corps assignment was just too daunting, so we quit, packed up, and went home. During our exit debriefing at Peace Corps headquarters in Washington, DC, shortly before Christmas, a young Peace Corps staffer berated us for being sissies and contract-breakers.

I ended with a sense of failure that was attenuated by a smooth re-entry to life in New York City and by high stature in the marketplace as a Returned Peace Corps Volunteer. The Peace Corps' "Third Goal" never really caught my imagination. During the two years that I taught grade school in New York, I published an article (my first) on tie dyeing as a geography class project, and I gave a few talks to Rotary Clubs. But living abroad in remote places became a continuous passion that has persisted until today. I got hooked by anthropology and got a Ph.D. after spending three years with Tibetan refugees in India and Nepal. Since then I have lived for many years in India, Nepal, Bangladesh, and Indonesia, working as a manager of development projects and, for a time, as a United Nations staffer. Although we are now divorced, Judith and I provided each other with comfort and companionship throughout our time in Sierra Leone and beyond.

# 20.

## Service in Kukuna

*Judith Kimmes Barker*

About half of our Peace Corps group was made up of married couples, many of us newly married after graduating from college. The Peace Corps figured that married couples could work together well in small villages in Sierra Leone.

We complained to the Peace Corps staff Washington about our poor training course at Hampton Institute, especially about the girls' portion. They agreed with us but said there was nothing they could do at that point. To get us properly acclimated to a tropical climate, and perhaps to make up for the poor quality of our training, the Peace Corps flew us to St. Croix for a few weeks before our departure to Sierra Leone. The men were learning construction skills by building a community center for refugees from the island of Vieques, near Puerto Rico. Aside from keeping house in the living complex already built for the refugees, we women didn't have much to do. We spent a lot of time with our wonderful language teachers, sometimes at the great beaches.

The Peace Corps figured that because David and I had worked so hard learning Temne, we could also learn Susu, so they assigned us to a Susu-speaking chiefdom. They did eventually give us some training in Susu, but by that time we had already learned some on our own.

Some of my fondest memories were of having the children sing. We would record their singing on our cassette player and then play it back for them. They were so delighted by this that we had to limit it to two nights a week. I taught them some simple kids' songs in English, which they easily learned and loved to sing. On many occasions, we had to wake up a few children at the end of one of these musical evenings because they had fallen asleep on one of our floor mats, which were like what the Susu people used for sleeping mats. The Susu are very gifted musically. The children used homemade instruments to serenade everyone in town; the adults would also entertain the village on full-moon nights with their more sophisticated instruments. There was also much dancing going on those nights. Everyone was delighted when I joined in the dance. Occasionally some women from next door would drop by in the evening, and occasionally, some men did also.

I tried to get women to hang their wet clothes on a clothes line instead of laying them on bushes to dry, where the tumba fly could lay its eggs in the fibers. Later the eggs would hatch, and the larvae would crawl into the skin of the host and create a skin ulcer that usually became infected. Since the American missionaries who had previously lived in Kukuna were away for most of our time there, I became the local expert and source of medical aid. I began collecting medical supplies from various sources. From the government hospital in Kambia, 35 miles away, I was able to procure some excellent medicines to clean and then to heal the lesions on children's legs and arms that had become infected by the native treatment of herbs and cow dung. My mother and her friends supplied me with bandage rolls made from their worn bed sheets. Their mail always got safely through because they had no value on the local market. One of the medicines allowed me to clean out the wound, usually over the course of two or more days. Then I could apply the healing medicine, always covering the wound with a clean bandage until it was completely healed. Sometimes the wounds were one or more centimeters deep. I was very busy.

Occasionally, I was able to get some meds from the Peace Corps doctor in Freetown, especially if they were out of date. Usually they were still effective. One time shortly after receiving some eye ointment from the Peace Corps, an epidemic of conjunctivitis broke out in Kukuna. Many people became infected and came to see me. I was able to apply the ointment and tell them not to touch their eyes and to come back to see me every morning and evening until they were cured. Everyone followed my directions, and they were all cured. Of course, I had to wash my hands after each treatment. There was never the possibility of allowing my patients to self-administer any of the medications. It was necessary for me to handle the procedures. Luckily, the epidemic came to an end without my getting infected or anyone's eyesight becoming damaged. Years later, when I had a student who lost one of her eyes by untreated pinkeye, I remembered my experience in the Peace Corps.

My most dramatic first-aid challenge came when a young man came to me for help. He accidentally cut his own arm with his machete while cutting the bush in preparation for burning it. He was bleeding profusely and in a state of shock. I was sure that he would require stitches. I applied direct pressure to the wound using one of our towels. I was able to stop the bleeding. Yes! Then I gave him some warm soup. He calmed down quite a bit and became relaxed. At that point, I heard a vehicle approaching, which was very unusual. Lorries would normally make the trip from Kukuna to Kambia each morning and return each evening. It was very rare to hear a car in the middle of the day. My patient was comfortable sitting on an armchair in my living room, so I went outside to the road. When the driver saw me, he was shocked, but he stopped. His passenger was a government official who needed to deliver a letter to the chief. I asked him to take my patient to the hospital in Kambia when he was finished with his official business, and he kindly agreed to do just that. There was a lot of blood to clean up, but there was a happy ending to that story. I was preparing myself to try stitching him up, but relieved that I didn't have to do so.

I often sat with neighbor women in their kitchen area and tried to communicate with them and play with their children. I also did some work at the school, mostly in nutrition education and helping them to use the surplus food from the U.S. such as lemon pudding and pancake mix. I also helped the children to practice their English.

The Peace Corps expected volunteers to look out for each other, and I think we did that quite well. The two PCVs who preceded us were generous in orienting us, and the Peace Corps teachers in Kambia opened their hearts and home to us many times. During our time in country our most frequent interactions were with Gerry Cashion, at the Kambia rest house, and Bob Galeria, posted to the neighboring Tambaka chiefdom. We periodically would ride with one of them down to Freetown to get supplies at Kingsway and a little R&R at the Peace Corps rest house and the Lebanese restaurant. I actually encountered one of my old boyfriends there. He was a professional photographer on assignment.

We took annual leave and traveled through West Africa. I contracted an infection and had excruciating pain while we were in Abidjan, Ivory Coast. The Peace Corps doctor was out of the country so I saw a doctor at the local hospital who gave me some pain suppressants rather than the antibiotics that I needed.

The end for us came in November 1966 in a typically Bramaia bittersweet way. Sheku S. Dumbuya, the only literate member of the chiefdom council and the only "modern" leader in the chiefdom, was elected paramount chief. We had pinned nearly all our hopes on him throughout our first months, but in May he had propositioned me, scaring us both enough that we dared not leave me alone for a night in Kukuna. Being paramount chief gave him such great new powers that we decided that we could not remain in Kukuna under any circumstances.

Over the course of the next few years after the Peace Corps, my infection prevented me from bearing children. It turned out well in the end, though. In 1975, David and I adopted Andrea, and in 1981, we adopted Susan, both of whom are now married and have children of their own. I continued teaching, for 35 years, from preschool to high school, in international schools in Nepal, Bangladesh, and Indonesia, as well as schools in the Washington, DC, area. My marriage to David ended in 1997. I am now retired and spend my time doing volunteer work and playing with the grandchildren.

# 21.

## A Midnight Adventure and...

*Tom Crum*

It has been 40-some years since I was in Sierra Leone, yet it seems like only yesterday. The faces of people in our group pass through my mind as I read through the roster of names. They are clear, fresh images, just as we were when we started our Peace Corps training at Hampton Institute in the late summer of 1965. How do they look now, I wonder? Are we still a band of brothers and sisters out to make the world a better place, or have we discarded our dreams along the way and exchanged them for the demands life placed in front of us, and in the process ceased to dream?

My Peace Corps experience has been like a filtering process, working its way through the years with me, always beside and within but never forgotten. It is like a compass built around two years of intense experiences that become clearer and more meaningful as the years pass.

Almost lost in the glow of living in Sierra Leone and being "overseas" is a very stark, simple fact: we chose to do it! What a risk it was, when viewed now, when security and performance have partially replaced the willingness to step off into the unknown. In our time, if I remember the numbers correctly, only one in five applicants actually became Peace Corps volunteers. And I recall the ambush of rejection at Hampton, when people were cut.

I gave up a very good job at the Boeing Company. A year out of college, it was a dream job that would have been very rewarding. But the dream was not the one inside my heart. Sitting at my desk one day and looking out across the huge office, about the size of two football fields that I shared with 5,000 other people, my little voice said, "This isn't going to work for the next 40 years." And so began the journey down that other road, the one "less traveled," as Robert Frost put it.

The courage to risk and live, at times boldly, is for me the biggest learned experience and gift of the Peace Corps years. In countless ways the sense of self-reliance and confidence, fostered and expanded by two years of experience in Sierra Leone, has been a main foundation of my post-Peace Corps life.

The list of experiences is endless, but two examples may serve to illustrate my point. The first one was on a night road trip with Gerry Cashion. We were coming back from a gathering at Makeni. We were not feeling any pain due to the refreshments enjoyed earlier. Gerry's Land Rover began running very warm. We halted, got out, and lifted the hood. It was hot all right. As we were in a state of reduced sobriety, we found that very funny. Can you picture two white guys standing in the middle of a jungle road bent over double with laughter?

Since the AAA was not around, we began to think that we did, indeed, have a problem. But being the resourceful Peace Corps volunteers that we were, we remembered the unopened case of beer we had in the back of the Land Rover. We proceeded to open up the beer and pour it into the radiator—and into ourselves. There were some other liquids added to the Land Rover radiator that night, but I will not get into that. It would have been a scene worthy of Monty Python: a jungle road with two loopy guys pouring beer into an overheated Land Rover.

You might be thinking that is not exactly an uplifting example of American care and concern for a Third World country, let alone a great life lesson. If you are, you have missed the point. Remember Apollo 13's serious problem on the far side of the moon? They fixed it with duct tape. Get beyond the boundaries of the situation to find a solution. You're not always going to find it in the book of directions.

For 25 years I worked as a home insulator with the business I started. From there, I gravitated toward rather extensive remodeling jobs, where not much was easily done or laid out in a do-it-yourself book. I did some pretty strange things over the 25 years, but they always worked. And the laughter of that night with Gerry Cashion was a reminder not to get too serious about just about everything.

The second of my experiences involved having motor problems with the boat the Peace Corps provided me. My then-wife Inger and I lived in Kychom, the headquarters town of Samu Chiefdom, in the Kambia District. The village was near the mouth of the Great Scarcies River. There were lots of tidal backwaters running between the rice fields. The tide was going out, so water deep enough to float the boat was shrinking. And it was getting dark. I did not have a flashlight, but it was a night with a full moon. The banks of the meandering channels were favorite resting places for crocodiles, so getting out of the boat to scout ahead was not a good option. The motor kept running, barely, and by trusting instincts and dead reckoning, I finally worked my way back to the river. The lights of my village were a very welcome sight as the faltering motor finally got me back "home." I do not recall being scared—a little anxious, perhaps—but not overcome with fear. It was a sticky situation to be certain, but confidence carried the day.

In the early 1990s, when my late wife Betty was dying of cancer, I experienced another night journey through very dangerous, and eventually fatal, territory. The night in the boat on the Great Scarsies River played a part in my determination to get past cancer and be the very best caregiver I could be. The unknown and unseen *were* scary but not incapacitating. Resolve comes from collective difficult experiences where one takes on the motto of the Seabees in World War II, "The difficult we do right away. The impossible takes a little longer."

I still dream of better things, but those dreams are tempered by 40-some years of experience. My wife Betty's death forced me to make more life changes, into more uncertainty, just like leaving Boeing for the Peace Corps. I started graduate school at age 50, got a master's degree in pastoral studies from Seattle University, worked as a hospital chaplain, and spent the last 14 years as a special-needs bus driver for the Bellevue Public Schools. I still have a dream of "better," but it's not quite as lofty as Saving the World, as I suspect we once thought we were going to do. It was a great time!

# Glossary

Bolli        Term used by Susu and Temne speakers to describe flat swampy grasslands that could quite easily be used to cultivate paddy rice.

Bonga        Small oceanic fish, dried by smoking and sunlight, traded widely throughout Sierra Leone and used as an important source of protein in *chop*.

Chop        Generic Krio term for cooked food, usually a stew.

CINVA-ram        A CINVA-ram is a lever-action mechanical press to make compressed earth blocks suitable for constructing simple durable buildings, developed in the 1950s by the Inter-American Housing Center (CINVA) in Colombia and adopted by the Peace Corps in the 1960s.

Court barre        A gazebo or bandstand-like structure typically built in the center of chiefdom headquarters towns and important sub-chiefdom villages, serving as a court during the daytime and an entertainment center at night. The paramount chief usually serves as magistrate for local court proceedings.

Expat        English-language slang for "expatriate."

| | |
|---|---|
| Juju | General European term used during the colonial period to designate African religious practices. |
| Krio | The Sierra Leonean variant of Creole English, originally spoken by former slaves resettled in Freetown, which gradually became the common second language of the country. |
| PCV | Peace Corps Volunteer. |
| Poda poda | Motorized urban transport vehicle used in Freetown. |
| Poto | Krio term for "foreigner." The word is derived from "Portuguese." |
| Pye dog | "Ownerless" "stray" mongrel dogs co-existing with people in villages throughout Africa, tolerated but often abused with sticks and stones. |
| Ramadan | The ninth month of the Islamic calendar, during which devout Muslims fast from dawn to dusk. |
| Sierra Leone Selection Trust (SLST) | Colonial-era diamond-mining monopoly nationalized in 1971. |
| Tief, Tiefman | Krio terms for "thief." |
| Vimto | Purple-colored carbonated soft drink manufactured in the UK and sold in glass bottles in towns throughout Sierra Leone in the 1960s. |

CPSIA information can be obtained at www.ICGtesting.com
Printed in the USA
LVOW011443150213

320307LV00003B/4/P